UNWEIRD

Angela Beverly

ISBN 978-1-64258-105-8 (paperback)
ISBN 978-1-64258-106-5 (digital)

Christian Faith Publishing, Inc.
832 Park Avenue
Meadville, PA 16335
www.christianfaithpublishing.com

Printed in the United States of America

This book is dedicated to single Christian women and men.

But I speak this by permission, and not of commandment.

For I would that all men were even as I myself. But every man hath his proper gift of God, one after this manner, and another after that.

I say therefore to the unmarried and widows, it is good for them if they abide even as I.

—Apostle Paul (1 Cor. 7:6–8)

TESTIMONY SERVICE

All I saw was white, and it was moving. I was clearly on my back as whiteness traveled directly above me. This couldn't be heaven, because there was nothing glorious about it. It was just bright, but not like Jesus being the "Light of the World" type of brightness, rather the type of shine that made me squint my eyes, so I closed them. I squeezed so tightly my eyelids began to ache and I could tell my facial expressions were dramatic. My head was the only thing in my body I could feel so I moved it right and left. I hoped the movement would wake me from this nightmare, *if* I was in fact dreaming. Then when that *wake-up* moment never happened, I tried to bury my head in something, but there was no covering or cushion. I wanted to scream, but I couldn't even open my mouth and I was now afraid to open my eyes out of sheer terror that I would see myself through some out of body experience struggling on whatever structure was transporting me. Was I floating? Was I being pushed? Dragged, or carried? I could not tell. Nor could I feel the rest of my body and my fear was elevated due to the utter silence. I felt bordered by extreme chaos but could hear nothing. My horizontal plane of movement soon transformed into spinning motions. The confusion from this episode made me gasp for air, I could no longer breathe and I believed I would pass out or die. I guess I just passed out because suddenly ... no, more like *finally*, I felt my eyes creeping open and I was not moving anymore. My breathing was normal again and I had the feeling I had been prayed for because there was such calm. I saw a woman hovering over me. She had huge eyes and they were green. I never saw eyes that big or green, but what stood out the most, was how much mascara she wore. It was what we refer to as tarantula eyes and it was freaking me out a little. Spiders nearly scared me to death and this woman's long glumpy eyelashes resembling spider legs was the last thing I needed to see at that moment. Her face was pleasant enough, but those eyelashes were killing me, so I shut mine to escape her form altogether. What happened to me and where was I? The last thing I remembered was testimony service during the New Year's Eve celebration at my church which we call Watch Night. I never liked New Year's Eve. Not because I celebrated at church, which is actually ideal for anyone who loves the Lord as I do. It was a fun time bringing in the New Year praising God! I don't like New Year's Eve for very personal reasons, which have everything to do with repeating this event year after year alone. All this time, I was uncertain if my friendship with Jasmine was wise. She believed in God, but she did not serve Him. But it was Tanner, my fellow Christian peer and friend who got the best of me. Or maybe … she got the worst of me. Now, here I am, trying to figure out where that is, knowing deep down, that I, Simone, am only to blame.

"When are you going to get married?"

ANGELA BEVERLY

"How come you don't have a boyfriend?"

"You're not dating anyone?"

"You sure spend a lot of time at church."

"You *still* don't have a boyfriend?"

"You must be picky."

"Are you seeing anyone?"

"As pretty as you are and you're not even dating?"

"I can't *believe* you don't have a boyfriend."

"You're telling me there aren't any guys out there for you?"

"I know you've met someone by now."

"When are you going to get married?"

REVELATIONS

Everyone has secrets. Things that only you and God know about you. My friend Tanner always left us wondering about her. Who was she really? She did not try to be mysterious, she just minded her own business and did not pry into yours. Yet, it made others curious. My friend Jasmine presented herself with no apologies. She was blunt about her position on everything. Gave the persona she had nothing to hide, you may have met the type. In the movies, she is sometimes the most suspicious one. I'm Simone. Not sure what people think of me exactly. Don't even know what to think of myself most times. God loves me. That I know for sure. Most days I think I'm normal, other days I feel like a weirdo. Thinking too hard on something can change you and your outlook on what's real. What was just a molehill becomes a mountain, and it did not have to be so. Tanner really knew how to make sense of things, so she was a go-to for chatting out those moments in life that took me by surprise. Jasmine makes me laugh and to hear her expound on a day at the office, can put you in stiches. But I had to be cautious with Jasmine, we did not feel the same way about a lot of things and I did not want to fall into her world of thinking. To get to the point, I discovered I had issues. Nothing out of the ordinary, so I thought. I had to come to terms with feelings and facts about those feelings. In a way, my friends had nothing to do with it, yet, somehow became the heart of it. Tanner wasn't my only go-to. My main go-to was God. Today, I needed Him before I even woke up. My eyelids slowly opened this morning but I wasn't sure if I was awake. My vision was low-def fighting for HD. Then I felt slobber on my pillow, and knew I was awake. *"When are you going to get married? Are you dating anyone?"* I could still hear the voices from my dream. The questions irritated me in my sleep as they did in real time and I did not like waking up feeling annoyed. My imagination was unquestionable. As much as I delighted in the Old Testament and visualized fine details of my greatest heroes and their stories, surely my dreams would star favored moments from the Bible. The distinguished Joseph and his great reveal to his brothers. Young David standing before his people and the Philistines as he asked, "For who is this uncircumcised Philistine, that he should defy the armies of the living God?" The rocks, sling, and great defeat of Goliath! The breath-taking Solomon's Temple and that *glorious* dedication ceremony. But my dreams are about people bugging me about marriage? As they did in the Bible, I wanted to rent my clothes! Tanner shared how she often dreamed of biblical times in her sleep, did she really? How could she? Why couldn't I? At this hour, it was well past the crack of dawn. My body doesn't do the crack of dawn, it is somehow on automatic for waking up any time after 9:00 AM. I managed to mumble, "Thank you for waking me up this morning, Lord." But the dream troubled me, I had to get those voices out of my head. I had to talk to God, I had to praise Him. I began a *thank you* tirade. "Thank you God for your protection through the night. Thank you for your grace and mercy. Thank you for your love and favor. Thank you for your patience. Thank you for your forgiveness. Thank you for the mind you have given me to want to live a holy life. Thank you for your Word that encourages me. Thank you for the Holy Ghost, who helps me, strengthens me, and comforts me. Thank you for loving me, dear God. Sometimes I *feel* all alone, like Elijah did that one time, but I know that you love me and will never leave me alone. Thank you that I know who I am, where I am, and that my thoughts are clear and not confused. Thank you for the power you have given me through your strength. All the wonderful things you do that I don't deserve at all. I can move because of your grace. My brain is correctly registering thoughts and feelings because of your grace. I don't have the power to do any of those things on my own, it all comes from your grace, and I appreciate those particular details. I just woke up, but I already feel like I have a funky attitude problem so please forgive me. Forgive me for anything I feel that's not right. Anything I've said, thought, or did against your will right down to negative expressions. Bless my family today, Lord. My friends, church, ministry, the leaders of this world, and let your will be done in my life even though I don't always know what that means or like how it feels. Help me to keep my mind on the ways of Philippians 4:8, so I can develop a spirit of worship toward you all day. I'm not concerned about tomorrow, I need to get through today."

I had to work on my prayer life and be more patient listening for God to speak back to me. I knew the benefits of a sincere and *consistent* prayer life not only reaped physical type blessings and special experiences, but also the type of blessings that could never be purchased with money. So, why was it difficult to commit to this beautiful practice when the payoff was so huge? I had come a long way from feeling trapped with *diseases*, like the woman with the issue of blood needing to get to the hem of Jesus's garment. It was important to lay a foundation of prayer and focus on spiritual things before the thoughts recaptured me. Later, in Super Walmart Simone walked like she knew where she was going headed toward the ice cream isle. When it feels it's just you on earth, something should be an option for company or a pleasant distraction that makes you feel loved. On her birthday, Simone devoured French Silk pie, as in *an entire pie*, and ice cream on New Year's Day. Simone was certain she would reach for her favorite mint chip, but a possible death by chocolate experience was considered, with chocolate chunks surrounded by chocolate ice cream, swamped with chocolate-covered almonds. But it was 1:00 AM, and that combination would be too rich at that hour and was dismissed. Vanilla would be as exciting as a cement wall, so she reflected on a childhood favorite in Neapolitan, but definitely needed something crunchy or chewy to take the lead. Vanilla with brownie chunks and caramel warped in between could do it. Simone stood there, looking from left to right, feeling lost in a crowd of flavors. She had no idea he stood behind her, patiently waiting for her to choose. "My favorite is the Oreo Cookies and Cream," he said. She blinked to clear her eyes and looked straight ahead. She could see his reflection through the cold glass door. Simone began to turn her body to face this man and it felt like she spanned in slow motion. His voice felt so familiar, though she was hearing it for the first time.

Her brown eyes met his brown eyes and his entire face smiled at her. "That is the dumbest thing I ever heard in my life." Jasmine cut her off before she could go on rambling about the ideal meeting with the man who would be her husband. Simone let out a frustrated sigh and shook her head at Jasmine. She was just getting to the juicy dialogue she would have with this gentleman, now her thoughts were lost. "Sounds like one of those unrealistic romantic comedies that make me want to throw up," Jasmine said.

"It could happen," Simone insisted. "Since I can't seem to meet him at church, I might as well meet him in the ice cream isle."

They both had a laugh at that one, but Jasmine insisted Simone get off her knight in shining armor dreams and quipped that "romance is for weak people who don't have the guts to live alone. True love is me and my freedom without some *needy* guy taking up my personal space whining about his empty box of Froot Loops."

With that Simone's jaw dropped and she believed Jasmine reached a new low on love. "I have news for you, Jasmine," said Simone.

"What news, Simone?" asked Jasmine.

"Out of all our single friends, you'll be the first one married," Jasmine quickly replied.

"Oh, that's another stupid scenario from the stupid romance movies, but I'm real-life friend. You know what would be ideal?" She did not wait for Simone to answer, "Men *really on* Mars. I mean, they're not good *for much*, and we're running things anyway, what difference would it make?"

Simone now needed coffee and wished for Tanner to make her entrance. They waited for her at Slow Sip Coffee, Simone's favorite café. At first she just wanted a blended mocha, but now she craved an espresso with a drip of cream to tame the turbulence but not so much to disturb the strength. She would need a jolt to counter Jasmine's animated comments contrary to her feelings.

"So, where is Tanner? Jasmine asked. "I was really hoping to meet her this time."

"I'm getting coffee," Simone said. "If she's not here in a few, I'll shoot her a text. Do you want coffee?"

"Not just yet."

Jasmine was really a cool chica. Simone always thought so. Her views on men were hardcore, and she cut Simone to the bone at times with her opinions, but she was the kind who would rush right over in the middle of the night without a second thought if there was a crisis. Simone viewed her as an unrepented version of Tanner from her recent discussion describing Jasmine to Tanner. "She's a former style of you!" Simone quipped, wagging her finger.

"Really," Tanner said. "You have me all figured out like that?" Tanner asked.

"Well, it seems level enough," Simone said. "Jasmine can be a bit wild, but she's not out of control." Simone finished.

"I'm a sinner saved by grace," Tanner said, "but I assure you my life before Christ wasn't as entertaining as Jasmine's life sounds, trust me."

Simone returned to Jasmine enlightened with her espresso. Happiness was a simple thing to Simone—a shaded seat at AT&T Park for a San Francisco Giants game, a pleasant walk in the Milpitas hills, as the chilled breeze made her hair dance, and at last, the perfect blend of coffee, whether it was her favorite white chocolate mocha or the edgy espresso she was about to slow sip on. She pulled her seat out and what happened next was an oh-no moment! Right-handed Simone switched the coffee to her left hand, to pull out her chair and somehow inadvertently crossed her feet before she would sit, and the espresso was tossed all over Jasmine and her runway-ready draped blouse! You could feel every head in the café turn in unison toward the scene as Simone gasped and the unfortunate meeting of espresso and silk took center stage. Everyone was halted like a mannequin in silence for about five seconds until some cute guy walked in and restored normality.

The next day Jasmine still e-mailed her usual late afternoon *General Hospital* update to Simone. She was distressed that her beloved Jason character was replaced by the former Billy from *The Young and the Restless*. "How could they do this?" she wrote. "You don't *replace* Jason! Put him in a coma and let him take a long vacation or something. It's the soaps, do anything but replace Jason! I just don't know if I'll be able to keep watching now." It took Simone by surprise that someone who hated cheesy romantic storylines was such a soap opera fan. "I blame my mother, grandmother, and babysitter growing up. They all watched *General Hospital,* how could I escape it?" Simone also wondered how in the world she religiously watched *General Hospital* from work every day! But most importantly, she was over the whole coffee spill incident. There were no hysterics, it happens. But of course, after that, Jasmine didn't stick around to meet Tanner. They both left shortly after Simone did what she could to prevent permanent damage to Jasmine's blouse. Simone knew she would call on Tanner right after she made it home. "What happened to you tonight?" Simone would ask. Tanner went in-depth about Bible study and how the discussion on "hope" was so good, everyone lost track of time. Then, about thirty minutes past the hour, they noticed Sis. Benjamin took off, so they must have gone over time. Someone could be speaking with all the eloquence and authority of Dr. Martin Luther King Jr., and the entire class caught up in the inspiration of the Word of God, and Sis. Benjamin will still leave on the dot, when Bible study was supposed to be over, period. Tanner shared thoughts and testimonies that were brought up in class and how someone began talking about hope for marriage. Tanner knew Simone wished to be married sooner than later, so she shared what she heard. How one church mother met her husband when she least expected it and he came way from the east coast, to her west coast, and they have been married for forty-six years. God had it all worked out for them. Sister Gray, who recently married, agreed, and believed God allowed her husband to find her after she earnestly prayed for a spouse and finally, Evangelist Cole wished to encourage all the singles and insisted you should want to marry. "She said that?" Simone asked, "you should want to be married?"

"Yep, that's what she said," Tanner remarked. "But the point of the lesson was not focused on marriage or any one thing in particular. It was about not losing hope for any prayers you have before God. Great points were brought up about our behavior and attitude while we're waiting for these blessings and keeping God's will the priority for our life. What I got the most out of it was the importance of enduring the waiting period without whining and including a spirit of praise to God in the process."

Simone went back to the marriage discussion. "Do you think everyone should *want* to be married?" she asked.

"I think folks who want to be married should marry and folks who wish to stay single should be single," said Tanner.

"Either way, you'll need God's help if it's your desire to please Him. To marry or not to marry, that sounds like a choice," Simone thought. At this point in her life she did not see it as a choice, only a desire. How could she see it as a choice, as if she could just go out and get married? As if it were simple as that. As if she could snap her fingers and a mate would appear. At times she felt she was blamed for not being married, it was her own fault. Some thought she did not go out enough to expose herself to single men. A few thought she should just go on one of those websites and find a compatible match. Others thought she was too particular, which always puzzled her. Shouldn't one be particular about the person they plan on spending the rest of their life with? It wasn't as if he had to be a perfect man with zero character flaws because she was not a perfect woman and it was not fair to expect from a mate what she could not offer in return, which was perfection. But the worst thought was any who may have believed she was gay. Why else was she not married at this point? The slightest notion of anyone thinking she was not attracted to men made her beyond uncomfortable. It also troubled her that divorce in the church among Christian couples was often. It disturbed her that some Christian couples she knew of were divorce specialists and on spouse number three. What was the problem with the saints who kept getting married and divorced? In the church, some pastor, evangelist, or prophet was always harping on being married, wanting you to be married, saying things like you *know* you want to be married, you should want to be married, and it will happen. No one praised the single life, except to say take advantage of that time with just you and the Lord *until* you get married. No one embraced the possibility that you may not marry at all, as if that was never a part of God's plan for anyone's life. It was always "don't worry, the Lord is going to bless you with a husband." So what's wrong with me then, why am I forty-three years old and still single?

The truth was … meeting men was very mysterious to Simone. She would notice a couple in the super market or observe married couples at a cookout or something and wonder how did they even get to that place? How did they actually meet, realize at some point there was an attraction, begin a dating period, fall in love, *she supposed,* and get married? Meeting men was like the magic trick she couldn't figure out. Where were they? They were not at her church. The married ones were, and then there were the single ones with serious issues still living with their mama. There was the single man who was loyal to church and living for Jesus, but old enough to be her grandpa. Then there was that single man who appeared to be most compatible—he was the right age range, saved and sanctified for sure now, but already had two ex-wives and six kids between the ages of five and nineteen. He found Jesus after two families, too late for Simone … or was she just *too particular*? Finally, someone with promise would show up. But you have to work fast in the church and be a bit shameless. There are tons of single women, but hardly enough of those single men to go around. If you were thinking about waiting until after church to attempt a flirt exchange with this man you've already lost him. The more desperate sister locked him up by the time the welcome address was given. She would find her way to his pew and cozy right next to him as if they were already a family. The practice of meeting men seemed simple for other women but completely foreign to her. Simone was unmarried and a part of her was ashamed of being unmarried. It was beginning to get to her.

NEW YEAR'S EVE

ew Year's Eve was coming and with it Simone would be
exposed. It was September, which represented fall, her
favorite season, but knots were tying in her gut as she
looked to endure the next three months leading to December 31.
Simone hated New Year's Eve as she hated her birthday. Hate is a
strong word, a negative word and she didn't like using it or feeling
it. She looked up the word hate—*to dislike intensely or passionately;
feel extreme aversion for or extreme hostility toward; detest.* She could
only conclude that was pretty much how she felt about New Year's
Eve and her birthday. She would not dare share her feelings regarding
these special occasions because it would sound too anti-Christian.
Simone caught up with Tanner who would spend her New Year's
Eve in Tampa, Florida, at MacDill Air Force Base. The adventures of
Tanner as a noncommissioned officer allowed her to travel to tem-
porary duty assignments from Canada to Norway and participate in
various exercises or training regimes, and she would still be assigned
in Florida as the festivities of a new year would dawn. Tanner likened
her military life to opening presents … anticipating moments full
of surprises. Tanner enjoyed the mystique of not knowing what was
in the box arriving in foreign countries and taking in a new culture.
Even within the United States prepping for Mississippi and professional upgrade training after growing up in the Bay Area and diversity
of California, she pondered what would be in the box of Mississippi?
Tanner's travels always ignited fascinating dialogue. She was dubbed
"The Rock Star" by her neighbor while living in Tajikistan for a year.
The locals eyeballed her every move strolling through the neighborhood to the local market until she was out of their sight. They took
her picture and wanted a picture with her. One young woman even

recorded her on her smartphone while she was eating in a restaurant. They weren't used to seeing black women there. Now, on the east coast was Tanner dwelling three months ahead dooming New Year's Eve? Hardly, Tanner was meeting new friends during her short-term work site. She was living in the moment and enjoying September in Tampa. Tanner was living in faith, she did not mind being an unmarried Christian woman, so bringing in a new year the same status she had at midnight, did not disrupt her psyche. Simone wished she was as strong as Tanner. She wished she could introduce Tanner to Jasmine, so the three of them could socialize together but occurrences always seemed to prevent that introduction … at least for the time being. Simone still carried on about Tanner to Jasmine when it was just the two of them out on one of the cool escapades Jasmine would come up with. "Don't you ever go anywhere besides work, home, church and church conventions?" Jasmine asked after the one thousandth time Simone invited Jasmine to join her at Bible study. "One of these times, I may surprise you by actually going to one of your church services. From Sunday to Monday, you guys have so many classes your members should turn in the training for meeting college credit requirements. I'm not knocking your faithful attendance, but there are other places you could go to you know." Jasmine insisted Simone join her for a San Francisco Food Street Festival that would cover four blocks in the Mission District of casual dining in a relaxed atmosphere with exquisite eats.

After nearly three hours of the perfect bite-sized plated provisions visiting vendor after vendor, Simone felt like that stray cat who adopted her yard sprawled under the tree without a care in the world. With a fresh minted icy tea infusion, Simone and Jasmine walked to Dolores Park nearby to people watch, chat, and continue their unwind day in the heart of the bay. "She just lives life, she's not hung up on status quos, expectations, marriage," Simone said.

"Tanner has the right idea," Jasmine said. "Now I could be wrong. But I imagine waking up to the same man every day is like waking up to that same zit on your forehead that just won't go away. Why would a woman want that?"

Simone was now past being stunned at Jasmine's blatant points of view. At this stage a softening in her tone toward marriage would shock her. "Most women don't think of men as zits, Jasmine. They think of them as potential husbands, fathers to their children, a friend, companion, and lover, someone to grow old with, kind things like that," Simone said.

"Hmm," Jasmine said. "That's awful nice of most women to think of them that way, but being single is the best thing since America was discovered! You said yourself how much you enjoyed the independence, no commitments. That could be forever."

"Sure," Simone countered. "I've enjoyed learning about independence. I was never in a hurry to marry you know? For me, entering my twenties didn't mean getting married, it meant begin to experience the big deal about being single! That didn't just include potential dates, but find out what I was made of. What I could and could not handle, my strengths and weaknesses. Understand my personality and moods. Realize if I wanted to pursue college or focus on a career or both? What do I even want for a career? Being single was more about self-discovery, understanding my individuality and then eventually meeting that guy after grasping the gist of who I was. I never wanted to go from my parent's home, directly to living with a husband. I wanted to know what was in between. I looked forward to having my own apartment and decorating it. I wanted to go home after work, to a place that was all my own. I wanted to understand the process of paying my own bills and the responsibilities that come with being a grown up. I wanted to know I could make it as a single adult, relying on God as my help and my upbringing for smart decisions. Is that so bad?" Simone wondered.

"No, I love it!" Jasmine exclaimed, "I'm getting excited, we finally agree on something. The experience is not overrated," Jasmine said.

"I loved it too," Simone confessed. "I enjoyed what I call light luxuries, like soaking in bubble baths without being bothered. Hanging out with my friends late nights without concerns of a family waiting for me or taking off on last minute trips without approval from a spouse. But it got old. After a while, I wanted someone to share my life with."

"Now that's where you lose me," Jasmine said. "You see, we handle loneliness differently. I don't care to share my life, but I don't mind sharing moments of it. I just get a boyfriend or a man who is a friend. I prefer the latter because they usually understand they're not sticking around. When we're done, you may leave. Boyfriends tend to think I still want their company afterward. So, there it is. Sex, just have sex. You'll be freed from the urge to marry in no time." Jasmine flipped her hair and quipped, "Woo-hoo! When was the last time you had a date or a boyfriend? You need to go out more and I don't mean a Bible study date at church."

"Back off," Simone said. "I don't fornicate. Christians don't fornicate."

"Really?" Jasmine asked. "My cousin's a Christian, she does it and I can't believe you used the word fornicate. I've only heard that word watching some type of documentary from the '50s or something. It's okay to say sex now, Simone, and like I said, I've met a few Christians who do it."

"Well, they're not a Christian according to the Bible, because it instructs about a thousand times that thou shalt not do it," Simone said.

"In this day and age, where everybody is doing a little bit of everybody, you expect people to be in a relationship and not do it? Jasmine asked.

"I expect people to do whatever they please," Simone said. "God gives us the freedom to make our own choices, if it rocks your boat to do it, then do it, but He also makes it very clear that if I choose to fornicate, I choose to sin. People will try to justify it all day and we can debate it all day, but it is written in black, white, and red and the position will never change according to the Word of God. Fornication. The word that means one is having sexual relations, but one is not married. This action is a sin. I know there are a lot of people out there doing it and I know there are so-called Christians doing it, but it doesn't make it right in the eyes of God."

"Well, now I know why you don't have a boyfriend and you'll never have one. Your sexuality has all the charm of a robot! For someone who wants to marry, you're way too safe. You're going to have to loosen up. If you're going to date a guy and intend on having a boyfriend, he's *going* to want to do it sooner than later," Jasmine said.

"I've had boyfriends, and I've had men who are friends and they all knew there would be no sex. I don't give mixed messages. I don't tell them I'm a Christian and then invite them over for a cozy candlelight dinner in a form fitting dress with my titties hanging out," Simone said.

"Yeah, that's probably what my cousin does," Jasmine laughed.

"Christian women and men for that matter can't just go hanging out with anyone," Simone said. "We have to be careful. Putting ourselves in a situation where we know we will be tempted sexually risks our whole relationship with Christ, threatens everything we believe in."

"You've had a boyfriend in this generation or decade?" Jasmine asked.

"What difference does it make? A boyfriend is a boyfriend. What does it matter when I had one last? Centuries ago, they wrote letters to their gal, now they text you or worse, send a tweet out to the world that they'll meet you at such and such a place, or they're breaking up with you. It's been over 2000 years, but men still have two arms, two legs, and a penis and unless he's my husband he ain't using his little ding-a-ling on me" Simone said.

"That *almost* sounds like something I would say, but you have a challenge before you if you want to be married without trying out the waters first," Jasmine said.

"The times have definitely changed, I realize that," Simone said. "The character of men has changed over the years, there are not as many gentlemen these days, but then there aren't as many women who carry themselves as a lady either. I haven't had a boyfriend in a long time, but that's okay. I'd rather be without a boyfriend and obey the scriptures than give in and offend Jesus Christ and myself. You know there is a man in the Bible named Joseph. Not Mary's Joseph, but this Joseph is in the Old Testament. His boss's wife wanted him bad and she repeatedly tried to get him to have sex with her. After he kept refusing her, she got so angry she cried rape. Joseph was falsely accused and thrown into prison. He would not have sex with her, not just because she was married, and not just because she was married to his boss, but because he cared about honoring the Word of God, he cared about honoring himself and he cared about how God thought of him. He did not want to let his boss down, he did not want to let himself down, but most importantly, he did not want to let God down. I appreciate Joseph and the stand he took to keep himself honorable."

"Well, Goody Two-shoes for Joseph," Jasmine replied.

Simone turned her head away from Jasmine, crossed one leg over the other and wilted into the tree trunk behind her. She rested her left arm over her head and looked onward toward the passersby and gentleness of the day. She gazed heavily into a leafy tree with pink flowers growing out of it. "I had my time with the boys though. It was the most fun years of my young life when I was a little girl and the most heartbreaking once I got older. Falling for a guy is so easy. The simplest thing can attract you to a man. His scent, his laugh, his voice, the way he wears his clothes, even freckles. You don't see too many black men with freckles, but I met this black man with freckles once. Never even knew his name, I had to help him right quick with a work issue. When I looked at his face and saw those freckles, it looked like someone sprinkled them on his face perfectly, as if each one was strategically placed right where they were supposed to be. It was a sexy moment. Did you know you could fall in love with a guy you don't even know?" Simone asked. Jasmine did not respond to Simone's question and was taken aback by Simone's feedback, and at once was at a loss for words. She just looked at Simone, realizing she was just as human as any woman who had passionate feelings for men. Most times she seemed a bit dopey or naive about men, but there in that instance, Jasmine felt Simone had loved and lost somehow or tried to. "Well, do you?" Simone looked sharply at Jasmine looking for her reply.

"I don't know. My goal is to never fall in love," Jasmine answered.

"Well, I'll tell you," Simone said. "You can fall in love with someone you don't even know. I know that to be very true." Simone insisted, looking back to her tree.

"Did you fall in love with the freckle-faced guy?" Jasmine asked.

"No," Simone said. "That all happened so fast. He appeared from out of nowhere, I helped him and he was gone. Never saw him again, even though I'll never forget those freckles."

Jasmine was not intrigued by lovey-dovey moments much, but she was fascinated with this insight on Simone, as if she were about to get some really good gossip. "Tell me about your boyfriends Simone," she said.

"Oh, like you said, it was generations ago. Since I've been a grown up, I've had male friends and gone out on dates. I've dated men I was fond of, was even attracted to a couple of them, and then there was that one. There's always that one guy who you'll never forget. The one that makes you think, what if?" Simone went silent into her daze again, and just as Jasmine would inquire about *that guy*, Simone snapped out of it and went back to her childhood memories. "But I feel like I lived my teenage years between eight and ten years old."

Jasmine's brow lifted. "That could mean a number of things if your teenage years were like mine," Jasmine said.

"Oh, it just means I was a wild little girl, a bit fearless at times. Then when I turned eleven," Simone paused for several seconds and looked lost. She didn't even blink her eyelids.

Finally, after what felt like an entire minute, Jasmine asked, "Well, what happened at eleven?" Jasmine asked.

"Absolutely nothing, everything seemed to fade," Simone said.

"What faded?"

"Every bit of confidence I had about myself and friendships, plus, I gave into a plain Jane look entering adolescence and it just got worse from there. My self-esteem was at an all-time low until I hit my twenties. I went from a pre-teen having boyfriends to watching all the cool kids and pretty girls hold hands and walk the high school yards arm and arm with all the guys I crushed on. In junior high and high school, I was known as the nice girl with the great personality

33

who went to church and wore long skirts. But it was fun having the boyfriends when I did as a girl. I felt cute and clever and brave. I was feminine enough to be flirty but had just enough tomboy in me to not come across as too fragile. I looked like a girl, behaved as a girl very naturally, but never shied away from getting dirty," Simone said.

"Who were your boyfriends?" Jasmine wanted to listen.

"Are you kidding me? That's going way back," Simone said.

"No, I'm not kidding, let's hear it. The crowds are leaving the festival by now and there will be tons of traffic. So, we can relax here and talk about boyfriends, or stay stalled on the 101 and talk about boyfriends. I'd rather do it here." She didn't just want some silly girl chatter, but whom and what once captured Simone's young girl heart and what else happened.

Boyfriends, Boy Friends, and Boys

" I had to be home before the streetlights came on and I could tell it would be dark soon, but I let Nina, the spoiled girl who lived on the third floor above us, talk me into going with her to see some guy she liked named Wilson. Now, Nina wouldn't get in trouble for getting home past the streetlights. She clearly held the strings over her parents. It was almost like they were scared of her. She yelled at them with no repercussions and even told them to shut up as she pleased. I knew I could never try that at home. Nina was cheerful, she was always smiling showing off the gap between her teeth. By the way, she punked her parents, I guess she had every reason to feel the world was at her fingertips. I remember her shoulder-length straight blonde mane and what was supposed to be some type of bangs, looked like a haircut gone wrong. We lived in a comfortable neighborhood of several apartment buildings which all had six floors, with six homes on the left side and six on the right. We set off to where we called the *other side* to see Wilson.

"It was identical to our end of living, but I didn't know anyone there, so I never went up that way. All of my friends lived in my immediate area that we just called *our side*. When we arrived at Wilson's building, there were no kids playing outside anymore because it was getting darker. We never went inside the building, Wilson and his little brother Cole came to the window to talk to us as if Wilson and Nina had some type of call code or something. How do you like that? The two guys were inside nice and cozy in their home, while the two dingbat girls stood outside in the dark talking to them through the window. They lived on the second floor like I did, so it was easy to see and hear them and realize they were both good-looking boys. I don't know which of Wilson and Cole's parents were black, but one of them clearly was, while the other clearly wasn't. Nina obviously pushed my attention toward Cole, who was just one year older than me, while Wilson and Nina were three years older than us. I do not recall much of what was spoken, besides the mention of some party and I remember Cole and me locking eyes and smiling at each other.

"Despite this intriguing tween meeting and new butterflies swirling about my heart, I had to get home because I was already in trouble … the streetlights were on. On our walk back, Nina filled me in on the party that would happen soon in the basement of our building and Cole would be there. As expected, my dad was waiting for me when I walked through the door and I was interrogated and punished. Now, my dad's idea of restriction was not like my friends' parents. When they were penalized, they could not go outside to play for a period of days, but I think my dad knew I could care less about not going outside to play. After all, I had the coolest Barbie doll setup in town right there in my room equipped with a three-story Barbie apartment with an elevator, barbeque set, and sports car. I also had my beloved Christie, a portable head figure with a small vanity attachment and I loved to experiment with fun hairstyles on her.

"Then there was my dad's cool music collection. I would sit on his stool in front of our gigantic shrunk, slap on his headphones and listen to '70s soul and my favorite Randy Crawford, Angela Bofil, and Teena Marie albums for hours. When the nine-year-old in me reared its head I pulled out a Charlie Brown's Christmas album. It didn't matter if it was winter, summer, spring, or fall, I welcomed this entertaining story year round and had it memorized. Where my dad got me was the dance at the youth center, which happened every other Friday night and I could not go to the upcoming dance, which was to take place in two days. Just grab a butcher knife and stick it through my gut. I only lived to go to the dance every other Friday night, but that Friday, I would stand outside and watch all of my friends and others walk right past me on their way to the dance. From then on the streetlights and I was in sync with our tune, before they turned on, I turned in. I was most grateful my father didn't know about the basement party that would happen in a week or so because then I may never have met Cole face to face. Cole was not my first boyfriend, but he always comes to mind first for some reason. The glow in his light brown eyes stood out and balanced well with is caramel skin. He had full lips and his hairstyle brought out an adorable scruffy puppy look about him. Cole wasn't shy at all and asked me if I wanted to dance with him.

"We spent most of the party dancing together, but I split my dancing time with some other guy who kept asking me to boogie whenever Cole stepped away. He always nabbed me back when he returned, which I loved. Cole started hanging out on our side after the party and some days later asked me to be his girlfriend. Our happy coupling was almost picture-perfect but there was a photo-bomber in our shot and her name was Tammie. As it turned out there were three of us in the relationship. I found out about Tammie, who must have found out about me, because she also began to visit our side stalking for Cole. I never got to the bottom of what Tammie was to Cole exactly except she was a girl he was very loyal to. It was as if she cast a spell on him because when she came a calling, he went a running and I was not cool with that. I didn't understand what Cole saw in Tammie. She looked like a dead girl walking and was bone thin. Her face looked sleepy all the time and her hair looked frazzled like her finger was stuck in a socket frying her brown tresses. Despite my harsh evaluation and feelings for Tammie, she had Cole wrapped around her finger, but I would not play second string. So long pretty brown eyes, I let Cole go," Simone said.

"Wow," Jasmine said. "What a cute story, I could just picture everything. Did he ever come back to visit your side?" Jasmine asked.

"No, I don't remember ever seeing Cole again, not even at school because he went to school number two and I went to school number one, which is how the schools were broken up," Simone said.

"Well, did you cry at all, I mean, you were nine, were you sad about this?"

"No," Simone replied. "I was upset about it, pissed in fact. I really liked Cole and wanted him to be *my* boyfriend, but even at nine, I was sure I wasn't going to split Cole with Tammie. There was something between them that he didn't have with me, but there were other boys in town, Cole wasn't the only fish in the pond."

"Who was next?" Jasmine asked.

"Taylor was next," Simone announced. "Unfortunately for me, he was never my boyfriend, but he was an incredible boy who was friend, and there is a great irony with our relationship."

"Spill it," Jasmine said.

"When my mother and I returned home from grocery shopping one day and I got out of the car, I heard a basketball pounding the ground and that got my attention. Taylor had this happy-go-lucky nature about him. He was headed my way from across the street pouncing that ball like an NBA champion and I figured he was going to the basketball court right next to my building. My friend Carly told me about the new boy on the block, on *our side*, and that had to be him. I don't remember how I formerly met Taylor, but Carly knew him first and there was no doubt she was whipped over him, but also completely defeated over the thought of a possible boyfriend scenario with him, as if he would never like her that way. I, on the other hand, could totally see me as his girlfriend, so with her sad *he'll never like me attitude*, I felt no fault in conquering our new friend or at least trying. The three of us along with three others all composed of three girls and three boys became inseparable nearly every day for a year.

"Once again, my age put me at a slight disadvantage which split us during school time because the five of them were one year older than me, which meant like Cole, they went to school number two, but after school and on weekends we were like sextuplets. I loved that Taylor always smelled like Ivory soap and his smile was like a lot of brown sugar in my bowl of oatmeal, so comforting. One of our favorite games to play on the basketball court was *around the world*, which I was pretty good at, especially from one particular spot where I never missed the net. Taylor was always first to applaud me and my biggest cheerleader during any of our varied games. Those were the days when we played on playgrounds and pushed each other on swings, enjoyed red light, green light, Simon says, tag, hide-and-go-seek, we made up games or just chased each other all over the place! We also had this great wooded forest behind the playground area and invented hunting style games and made our idea of weapons from the sticks and branches. I introduced them to one of our favorite games mean Mariah taught me called 7-up. This game only required a wall, and a tennis ball, so we used the side wall from any of our apartment buildings for that one.

"Taylor was a humble winner and good sport when he lost any game. His attitude, support, and friendship felt like a warm blanket, but if he was attracted to me at all, he never showed it. What I knew for sure, was that he liked a girl with one of them hard to pronounce—Shaunickalia, LaNicayqua, Rashoonda—names. Something like that. This girl knew how to roll her eyes and twirl her neck real good and she had strait attitude problems from birth. Her small clique included two other girls just like her, and that brat little kid sister, who learned her big sister's wicked ways, right down to the hands-on-the-hips routine. I never spoke to this girl, but she stared me down every time we crossed paths. She and her evil followers lived on the other side and stayed on their turf, but it was during that dance at the youth center every other Friday night, where we all met up, it was there, her friends would brag out loud so I could hear them say things like how much Taylor liked their girl, and it was there, she would seize Taylor's affection. She was cute. She had long hair that she flipped to the side and wore in a twisted ponytail most of the time. I saw Taylor staring and flirting with her, but never more than that.

"At their school number two I heard it was just more of the same. Always flirting, never touching. At the dance, what surprised me most with all their sickening admiration was that Taylor didn't seem to have the guts to dance with her, but he had no problems dancing with me, which always wiped the smug expressions off all their faces. Regardless, I wanted Taylor to look at me the way he looked at her. But despite the fact that he talked to her at school and came across as Romeo in love at the dance I managed to have the upper hand. Once the music stopped at the dance and the bell rang at school, Taylor played with me for the rest of the day. That's why, if looks could kill, that girl would've taken me out when I was ten years old. It turned out, I was to that girl, what Cole's Tammie was to me and I loved it, the end," Simone said.

Jasmine howled in laughter and said, "You're making this all up to make me feel good and believe you were this daring girl with a little wicked in you."

"Impossible, I couldn't possibly make this up," Simone said. "C'mon now, you know we were all like those girls at some point in our childhood, stuck up, jealous, mean, attitude overload. It came out in our pre-teen years, or adolescence, or college years. The goal was to grow out of it eventually, but some of us carried it right into adulthood and are still trippin'."

"So, that's it? Taylor never looked at you that way?" Jasmine hoped.

"Never," Simone admitted. "He looked at me with affection, but never affection combined with attraction."

"Keep going," Jasmine said. "Who was the next character in your movie?"

"Uh-oh. The next one is a little risqué and it really makes me wonder if I behaved with Jeremy the way I did in 1981 at ten, how in the world are ten-year-olds behaving now? I mean, back then the worst thing kids got busted doing was looking at some dirty magazine with their mouth open and eyes as big as their face from what they saw," Simone said.

Jasmine raised herself up from her elbows to her hands with keen interest and let her face do the talking. "How were you behaving, Simone?" Jasmine asked.

"Well, I don't know. I have to rethink this one. Some things you shouldn't share, you know. You might think I was a little girl whore," Simone said.

"I wouldn't put it past me. Go on," Jasmine insisted.

"I had more charm than a robot, that's for sure," Simone said. "Things got a little extreme and there was a bit of trouble, but in the end I was able to tame the naughtiness. Just want you to know that upfront before you judge me, I was a kid for crying out loud."

"I'm listening," Jasmine said.

"We were having this great picnic barbeque type thing in that large outdoor space behind the building. The mood was very relaxed. The wives were laid out on blankets, talking and laughing and the husbands were standing around the grill smoking cigarettes and drinking beer. I never thought of Jeremy as anything more than exactly what he was, my mom's co-worker's kid. They were over quite a bit because we always had get-togethers like that. I was used to playing with Jeremy during these parties for the last two years. He was really good at flipping off the bars and I would try to copy him, but always chickened out on those really big flips and release stunts where his landing would be at least eight to ten feet out from the bars. I stuck with my usual two or three moves swooping my entire body up, under, and back over the bar and would release for my landing pretty much directly under the bar not more than a foot away. Now, I was great at jumping a good distance off the swings, but I could never master the long distance releases from the bars like Jeremy. Usually, these gatherings were in the house with the kids outside playing, coming in and out periodically to munch throughout the day. This time everyone was outside, which left an empty house. I honestly don't remember why we ended up in my parent's room sitting on their bed watching *The Incredible Hulk* or why we weren't in the living room watching it, where there was also a TV.

"But there we sat and that's where it happened. I was introduced to rough kissing, necking, and the evidence that revealed it all … the lust-laden hickies! My goodness, horror stalked every nerve in my body upon discovery. How did this happen? Jeremy kissed my mouth and neck really hard. I kissed him back but had to come up for air. It all stopped for a moment when he asked to see my boobies and I remember looking at him like he was crazy. I had already crossed the line, there was no way I was showing him my boobies that actually did not exist anyway. I didn't even have enough going on to wear a training bra. After I refused to show off my teeny-weeny girlfriends, we started kissing again. When I came up for air the second time, I remember I could clearly see my reflection through my mother's huge bay window style vanity mirrors and that's when I realized what used to be an innocent neck was covered with red and purplish spots that looked like bruises!

"The period between my discovery of the hickies and my mother discovering them is a complete wash. All I remember next is me going to bed way earlier than I usually did, and praying that my parents would leave me alone. My hope was the hickies would be gone by morning and I could get on with my little kid life. So, I'm in my pink jammies lying in bed with my covers practically over my entire body. Then she called for me and I thought I would have a panic attack. At first I did not respond and in hindsight, I should've continued to ignore her, made her come to me, faked I was terribly ill all curled up or pretended I was asleep, something like that. Instead, I grabbed my robe, pulled the collar up and carefully wandered into the kitchen where she was. It felt like high noon in the middle of a desert in there, with the lights appearing much brighter than they usually did. My mother wondered what I was doing and why I was in my pajamas so early. I just stood there looking kind of dumb as she zeroed in on my neck, I was busted.

"Throughout my entire life, it was obvious my parents were never comfortable with talking to us kids about anything sexual. That's probably why I did not get in trouble for this. They would've had to address sex with me somehow and they didn't know how to do that. My goodness, if it wasn't for the sex education classes at school and the YWCC classes at my church, I wouldn't have known anything about sex at all! All I can remember after my neck examination is my mom telling me to go on back to bed and I never saw Jeremy again."

This story made Jasmine laugh again. She shook her head and held her forehead with her fingertips. "At least I was thirteen before I started kissing boys, Simone. Fast little Simone." Jasmine snickered.

"Let's just move on to Kyle, cause he won't take long," Simone said.

"Wow," Jasmine said. "What number are we on now? How many little freaks did you have? Were you ten with all these guys?" Jasmine asked.

"Eight to ten. I told you I felt like I lived my teenage years between eight and ten remember? I also kinda went backward, Kyle wasn't even my first boyfriend, he was before Cole, but after Brent. There isn't much to say about Kyle because we didn't stay together very long and he broke up with me. Kyle's older brother Kristopher was actually a part of my sextuplet friend group with Taylor. Kyle and I were the same age, so we both attended elementary school number one and we were both in Mrs. Larson's class. We had to have met there because I only remember us being together at school. He was simply the epitome of nice and proper. Unless he changed into some wild adolescent as a teenager, we would've been perfect together after I hit my teens, but the contrast in our demeanor was probably too much for him. Two things I'll never forget with Kyle. He bought me a brownie at our school bake sale, and even after he clearly wasn't my boyfriend anymore, he was still very kind to me. I don't recall much else about us. Maybe Kyle was just a rebound guy because of Brent, my very first boyfriend at eight years old.

"We actually had what we famously call an on-again off-again relationship for just over a year. Brent was blond as the sun and a die-hard Miami Dolphins fan. Whether it was a hat, shirt, scarf, jacket, he always wore something representing Dolphins sportswear and swore he would be their quarterback someday. It was embarrassing dancing with him at the Friday night youth parties because his dance style was … well, the only word I can think of is stiff. It was void of any type of emotion, and looked rushed as if he were always ahead of the beat to the songs. Since he was my boyfriend I thought I should dance with him, whether he was good at it or not. While we both attended school number one, Brent lived on the other side but he would come on down to my side to visit me. Most of our time together was spent on the school grounds where he played practical jokes on our friends, pushed me high on the swings and spun me on the merry-go-round.

"He had a lot of energy at school, while we were outside, we ran around more then we walked anywhere. Sometimes, he was too silly though, which led to our breaking up at times, but we always got back together. He kissed me once outside the dance. That would be our one and only kiss. It was just a quick smooch on the lips and he seemed pretty nervous about the whole thing, so we left it at that. Before our final off-again phase, I noticed he stared at Laura quite a bit. She was a dark-haired mild-mannered white girl and a good classmate of mine. I liked Laura. She reminded me of a female Kyle, she would've been perfect for Kyle, because Brent was wild like me. I felt like it was finally the end for me and Brent once he took notice of Laura. We were bored with each other once and for all and when we called it quits for good, there wasn't anything strange about it. I don't know if Laura and Brent ever hooked up. They never talked at school, maybe she lived on the other side with him and they became friends there. I never asked Laura if she liked Brent the way he seemed to like her and we remained friends even though we only hung out at school. During that time, there was only one other guy I crushed on after I believed nothing would become of me and Taylor. It was the most awkward, because everything about it was one-sided. Shayne didn't know I was alive.

"His homeroom was across the hall from mine and with every Wednesday morning, came all the excitement of a Christmas day. Each week our classes were combined on Wednesday and I'm certain that is partly what contributed to the worse school year of my life. I have no idea what was taught in class on Wednesdays, all I did was *stare stalk* Shayne and observe how he was head over heels with the girl who wore a braid in her hair. That was the only memorable thing to me about that girl. Every single day she had a braid one way or another. If I was smarter then, I would've worn a braid in mine, maybe he liked braids! Shayne's two front teeth were huge but some-how complimented his face when he smiled. The only two things imperfect about Shayne was that he sometimes wore pants a little too high water and his constant shadow, the girl with the braid.

"On my walk home, I would pass Shayne's apartment build-ing, which was across the street from the school and on the same left side of the street as my building, but a good six or eight blocks away. The only other time I walked past Shayne's building was the rare Saturdays Alice, Jon, and I would go to the bowling alley. If you looked at the front of his building, he lived on the first floor on the right side. I always walked as slow as I could past his building hoping to get a glimpse of him. The front entrance doors were glass and usually always open.

"If I didn't see him outside, I hoped he would be lounging around in the stairwell. Some days I lucked out. I wonder what became of those boys. What do they look like now? What did they choose for a career? Did they think of me ever again? Surely they're all married with children. Between Brent, my first boyfriend, and Shayne, my last crush it seemed a lifetime before I liked a guy again." Simone ended.

"What about the teenage and grown-up boyfriends?" Jasmine asked.

"Trust me," Simone said, "the little kid relationships were way more exciting! I'll tell you about them another day. The traffic should be cleared up a bit by now, don't you think?"

THEN CAME TANNER

Who knew mean Mariah's antics would have such an affect? It is incredible how one incident from childhood carries over into adulthood crippling your views about others. Simone could tell from the jump Mariah was wishy-washy. She was the type of friend who only liked you on her terms when she felt like it. But moving into the new town, Simone had no friends, so Mariah was it for the time being. She was the youngest of three, who had an older sister and the brother who was the eldest. They were a cute little sibling group, very close-knit. Mariah's mom was a housewife and must have been a total clean freak because there was this wide long sheepskin rug that covered the *entire* hallway from the front entrance of the door straight down to the master bedroom. Simone knew that was the master because all of the apartments were designed with the same wide hall path that looked as long as a bowl-ing lane, three bedrooms, huge living room, big kitchen and one decent-sized bathroom in the same setting as all of the other apart-ments. Although the master was intended for the parents, Mariah and her sister shared that bigger space, while the son and parents took the other two smaller rooms. Of course, everyone would have to take off their shoes before entering their home and stepping foot on that gorgeous sheepskin rug. Simone was invited in once, which is how she knew about the girls holding the master. So, it happened one sunny afternoon that shook Simone's eight-year-old core.

The one thing Simone admired about Mariah was her girlish appearance in contrast to her more tomboyish look. Simone loved her tight corduroys and sneakers and wasn't quite ready to jump into a world of cute flowered skirts, however, seeing Mariah adorned in such feminine charm all the time, made her question if she should adjust her style to look more girly. Simone rambled through her closet looking for pastel-colored clothing that would mimic a Mariah type look and she discovered an adorable pale pink skirt with flowers, paired it with a matching pink top, slapped on some sandals and was pretty excited to show Mariah her new style. Simone felt so good, she skipped over to Mariah's building, jogged up the five steps to the first floor and knocked on the door. Mariah opened the door and Simone could tell she was taken aback by what she saw. She kind of leaned back a little and quickly examined Simone up and down with her eyes then *exploded* with laughter. She was sincerely amused at Simone's expense to the point that her eyes watered and she called her sister Lydia to join in the fun. Their roaring laughter echoed throughout the stairwell, and Mariah began to slap her thigh the way you do when you're laughing so hard, you can barely stand it.

Lydia was bent over resting her hands on her knees, and after they were satisfied with Simone as the joke of the day, Mariah simply slammed the door in her face. Simone just stood there in total shock still hearing them laugh behind the door. She doesn't remember how long she stood before flopping down on the stair, and then she doesn't recall how long she sat before feeling her legs beneath her, getting up and walking back home. By the time Simone made it to her apartment, she had somewhat come to herself. She already felt a bit uncomfortable in the outfit to begin with, but now it felt outright icky and she had to get out of those clothes which obviously did not reflect who she was at the time. Simone put her corduroys back on and went outside to play, as if nothing ever happened, but she was wounded. She grasped two things from that incident.

First, she felt she did something she should not have done. Her eight-year-old mind struggled with the lesson, she could not quite put her finger on it, but it had something to do with being herself. She would fully understand many years later. Second, when she cut someone out of her life, they were out for good. The door was locked. Simone never spoke to or played with Mariah again. Did that influence how Simone felt about women getting too close, trusting them in friendship? She wasn't sure, but she never forgot the bleeding from that experience as it lingered in the back of her mind. She kept her girlfriends at an arm's length, wondering if they would turn out like mean Mariah. Two years later, Simone thought she could let her guard down when she returned to her grandparents' home to spend the summer. Thanks in part, to her obsession with Shayne and her below standard grades from the fifth grade, Simone had to attend summer school to make up for her poor ratings. She was pleasantly surprised to bump into the first friend she ever had outside of her cousins. Her name was Chloe. She lived on the same street as her grandparents and Simone couldn't wait to hang out with Chloe again, especially after the reunion with her cousins did not play out as she thought it would.

Time took its toll on a number of things. As always, she was the youngest among this group of first cousins. When she left, they were all kids, doing kid things. Playing marbles and jacks, collecting change from whoever they could to visit the candy man's house, chasing after ice cream trucks, making mud pies in the driveway, singing songs about Giant Robot and playing with cousin Michael's pigeons in the backyard. Four years later, at ten, she's still a kid, but they were all teenagers doing teenager things. They were clearly out of her league. But surely things would be the same with Chloe. On her way to math class, the sun shined brighter once Simone realized that was Chloe she was approaching in her path! Simone could immediately tell that Chloe recognized her too. She smiled and started walking faster to meet her friend. Leaned against a pole, Chloe was chatting with some other girls, she hadn't changed a bit, except she was taller.

Simone was sure she was about to hook up with her long-lost pal, and make new ones with the other girls in Chloe's clique. But the sunshine Simone felt was about to turn into an ice storm. The chills grew as she got closer to the group, and her face turned from a smile to a confused puckered brow. Chloe was not presenting any type of warm reception at all. The look on her face did not say, "Hey, friend, great to see you again," but instead it read, "what is she doing back here?" Chloe turned away discarding Simone's presence. Finally, Simone stood about two feet away from her and said, "Hi, Chloe." She did not respond with words.

Chloe looked at Simone, let out an annoyed sigh, tightened her eyes, her top lip slit up to one side like Elvis, and she turned her attention back to her friends. Her body language was expressive enough and it said a bunch of expletives in Simone's face. She didn't understand, what the heck was her problem? What had Simone done to deserve that? It was a long summer with Chloe's cold shoulder at school and Simone simply scratched her from her friends list. She had roller-coaster friendships with females throughout junior high and high school she just wasn't good at it. By the time she made it to DeAnza Junior College, it was with Rainey that Simone realized her lack of friendships was to some extent due to her own antisocial behavioral problems. Rainey was a lighthearted extrovert and Simone was a loner who overthought everything. Rainey's joy should have been contagious and rubbed off on Simone, but instead it was overwhelming and pushed her away. This was a problem that did not sit well with Simone's spirit.

She was a Christian, why wasn't she happy? Rainey was a ball of fun energy, and likely needed or enjoyed feeding off the same vigor and kindness from others that she so freely gave. To put it bluntly, Simone blew it with Rainey. Day after day, Rainey would find Simone in the cafeteria, library, or outside sitting on one of the benches somewhere, and certainly Simone's stand-offish manner could be felt. Sometimes Rainey's smile was so cheerful, Simone could not help but to relax and join in, but most times, she just could not return the thoughtfulness Rainey naturally shared. After a while, Rainey disappeared into thin air. At first Simone did not notice because she was caught up in her own lonesome world, but then she realized she had not seen Rainey in some days. She sat in the same place at the library and cafeteria, so Rainey could not miss her.

Then it hit her like a ton of bricks that she probably ran Rainey away. One can only take so much of a down-in-the-dumps type of friend. The desertion of Rainey triggered a spiritual and emotional self-evaluation. Simone sought the Lord and asked for His help to be more sociable and friendly, but she did not think to ask Him for joy and why she had so little of it. She would be forced to face that later. Nonetheless, she identified her negative I-don't-care-to-be-bothered vibe and made great efforts to adjust her disposition and be more approachable. She would never repeat the ugly nature she displayed with Rainey who could have been a lifelong friend. Simone was never comfortable in social settings, and had a knack for making awful first impressions, but as she got older and entered the work force, she became less uptight and began to focus on what she did right. Simone loved being a businesswoman. On the job her communication skills improved as well as her nonverbals because successful career principals included outstanding customer service, so she became more conscious of her expressions and tone. All of these garnered great relations with her associates, however, she still struggled with making true friends. At first she was underwhelmed, then she overdid it with new people she met, always aware of the mistake she made with Rainey.

Simone needed to find balance receiving and approaching others as well as establishing and maintaining honest, friendly relationships. Her friend span zone was all over the place, never consistent, but she had two breaks that gave her short-term hope and made her forget about mean Mariah. Although brief, she would be forever grateful for dear Rachelle and crazy Chelsea for at least the experience and pleasant memories of having girlfriends once. After the dreadful summer of Chloe and settling into her new family home in San Jose and the sixth grade where she made up for fifth grade by making the honor roll, Simone got through the awkward scenes of middle school because of Rachelle.

Boys were so mean in the sixth grade and looking back, Simone supposed they were going through growing pains and body changes just as girls were. Hanging out with Sheila and Serena wasn't working out. They had this air of coolness and boldness that Simone did not have. They didn't seem to mind that Simone kind of cramped their style, but she could no longer endure their popularity to her more private nature. The entourage during breaks and lunch time with girls picking fights with her because she was different was not what she was looking for in friend groups. Simone found Rachelle walking home from school one day, strolling down the same route to their homes and they just started talking. Rachelle was easy like

Sunday morning and there was nothing suspicious about her. Taking their time, it was about a fifteen-minute walk from the school to Rachelle's house, then another fifteen minutes from Rachelle's house to Simone's. They enjoyed their walks home talking about music mostly and who was on the cover of the latest *Right On* magazine.

On Saturdays they would visit the shopping center and walk through Montgomery Wards and always eat at Round Table pizza before heading back home. Rachelle would help Simone recover from the boy bashing and taunting about her new breast size that had grown out since the days of Jeremy. They would spend the night over each other's house some weekends, polish each other's nails, experiment putting on makeup that neither Simone's mother or Rachelle's grandmother would allow them to wear out to school or the shopping center, and talk about the boys at school they actually thought were cute. Rachelle lived with her grandmother and uncle and Simone was so saddened with the news that Rachelle's grandmother died because they were so close and it meant Rachelle would now have to move out of state to live with other family.

They wrote letters to each other for about a year, and then Simone no longer received any returns from Rachelle even after sending multiple letters looking for a response. Simone hoped she was okay and that she stayed the same sweet Rachelle she knew. In the last letter she received from Rachelle, she mentioned something about being a boy's toy. Simone did not like the tone of that and hoped she wasn't becoming a fast girl. She would never hear from Rachelle again although she thought of her often with great fondness. Between seventh and ninth grade Simone returned to being a complete recluse spending more time in the library than anyone except the by-the-book librarian officials who went around telling everybody to *shhh,* the second someone spewed out one word to another sitting next to them.

Simone did not have that worry since she was always by herself, but got a good *quiet* laugh over it whenever a librarian suddenly appeared in someone's face or behind them telling them to *shhh!* During Simone's sophomore year, she had the big personality of Chelsea as her best friend. They could not be more opposite. If

Chelsea loved it, Simone hated it and vice versa, yet they had a blast together! They went to the same church but never spoke there.

After breaking the ice at school, Chelsea told Simone she thought she was stuck-up because she never spoke to her and Simone confessed to Chelsea she never spoke to her because she thought she was rude and would be mean to her. Simone discovered that Chelsea was honest, but far from mean and she introduced Simone to leaving the high school grounds for lunch thanks to some boys she knew and one of them had a car. Simone felt cool for the first time heading to McDonalds for lunch just like the seniors did which was all the rave. Chelsea also introduced Simone to something she did not realize she lacked, which would change her life forever and that was the graceful act of sharing.

Chelsea was a middle child with an older sister, younger sister, and younger brother all raised by a single mother. Growing up sharing was inevitable and a natural action for Chelsea. Simone grew up with an older brother, two working parents, and pretty good provisions. She always had her own room and her own stuff, which meant she never had to share anything. But one day, Simone forgot to get lunch money and was at peace with the idea that she would just miss lunch. Chelsea wouldn't hear of it. She insisted Simone choose the lunch, choose which of the two drinks she wanted that came with the meal, and then they split everything else in half. Simone was amazed at Chelsea's kindness and ashamed that she would have never thought to share at all. She was hopeful for the chance to return the favor someday, which ultimately did come and Simone was honored to share with the friend who taught her to share with others.

Surely, they would graduate together and be best friends for life, but similar to Rachelle's arrangement, Chelsea too would move out of the state with her family after their sophomore year. Simone and Chelsea stayed in touch over the years and even visited each other a few times as adults, but the long distance between them turned into poor communication as their lives took on higher education, the corporate world, and eventually, marriage and a family for Chelsea. Geez, even discovering and keeping a home girl was complicated, or was she making it all complicated? She had no idea. As it went,

Simone constantly found comfort in the Word of God. She compared every feeling she had with how it coincided with the Word of God. She also found friendship there, literally. The friendship between God and Moses brought Simone to tears in a good way. She loved how God took up for Moses and would have done anything for him as he often times struggled with the task of leading the children of Israel. She loved when Moses wanted to see God in His glory and asked for this privilege.

Unfortunately, in his human body, Moses could not possibly see God like that and live, but Simone appreciated how God honored his request by shielding him in the cliff and allowed His glory to pass by while Moses could witness His back parts. Simone adored the friendship between David and Jonathan. Two men who simply loved and respected the other for the courage they demonstrated and loyalty in keeping their promises to one another. They were a lot alike as brave warriors who did the right thing although others desired them to do evil. Naomi and Ruth had a unique friendship which boiled down to the nitty-gritty of a life-altering decision. Ruth absolutely refused to leave the side of her mother-in-law and the spiritual rapport she developed with her and the one true God. Isaac and Rebekah's refreshing story unfolded friendship between young sweethearts and a rare vision of romance from the Bible days between newlyweds.

The touching incident with Jesus and the adulterous woman wasn't so much a friendship as it was an extreme act of friendship. The gentle Savior in the midst of mad men extended forgiveness rather than judgment and won a lifelong friend to this woman. So, friendships were not new and there were various examples of them even in the Bible. It was important for Simone to have friends, and she believed her lack of friendships contributed to the loneliness she felt and desire to marry for a bond with her husband who would be her best friend forever. She had her idea of the ideal friend. You were the best friend ever if you were loyal, could engage in Bible discussions, talk sports and Al Pacino films, and discuss politics without getting all weird. If you were too hard on King David, completely unreasonable regarding California sports teams, never saw The Godfather, or thought it was overrated, you just might be *unfriended*.

In the end, Tanner's friendship requirements really boiled down to loyalty. She would be a loyal friend and just wanted the same in return. Five years before she met Jasmine, there was Tanner. Simone already felt like the Elephant Man for being unmarried at forty, how could she not have a best friend too? Tanner comfortably fit into Simone's world. They were both COGIC women who understood committing to the truth in the Word of God. Tanner was preferential to the gentleman Joseph over Simone's complex David, but they could go on for hours exploring the Bible all day. Check. Tanner was not only from Simone's beloved California, but was also a huge sports fan! Simone did not hold it against her that she was from Southern California, born in Compton, as a Raiders and Dodgers fan. It was that much more fun that her Giants kept winning the World Series and Tanner's Dodgers kept getting eliminated in the playoffs. Check.

Tanner had not seen all of Al Pacino's movies but could recognize and analyze good acting, writing, directing, casting, and the perfect musical score in a film. Check. She wasn't so far right and too far left when it came to politics, she held to her own convictions with a level head about the controversial news topics, which equaled common sense notions. Check. Tanner was a keeper, she had to be her homegirl. It was most appropriate that Simone met Tanner on her birthday, the other blessed occasion she hated that she hated. She did not hate growing a year older, she was grateful for that part and tried to make it a celebration of thanks for knowing Christ, but it started with that question everyone asks, "What are you doing for your birthday?" Most women would be hanging out with their boyfriend, husband, or circle of friends. Simone had neither and it was embarrassing to confess she would be spending it alone.

The last time Simone had a birthday party was for her ninth birthday. After that she had a pleasant twenty-second birthday dinner when her mother prepared her favorite meal in the whole word, meatloaf and mashed potatoes, for the two of them. The older she got, the more she kept her birthday a secret from others because then they would know her age and be shocked that she was that old, never married and childless. At least it happened less and less as the years went by, but from time to time, Simone still met that person whose entire body froze with the mouth open and blank creepy stare when she answered, "No, I'm not married." Only for it to happen all over again for the next response, "Nope, I don't have kids either." Simone did not like hanging out with married folks or single parents.

They had too little in common, and were often preoccupied one way or another concerning their family matters. She did not know how to respond to husband and children talk, plus, it served as a hurtful reminder that she may never marry or have children. Tanner was the perfect friend, she was reliable, single, childless, and Christian, but she also upheld something else Simone needed—a strong contented approach to her single status that Simone wished to embrace to aid removing the heartbreaks of loneliness. Addicts always mentioned how giving into their addiction became that fix easing the pain in their lowest moments, and Tanner was like a drug. So, without thought as to how this would affect her spiritual life, and dismissing the lesson of mean Mariah, she became Tanner.

HIDING PLACE

If Jasmine heard "Santa Baby" one more time from her car radio, she was going to drive into a wall. Even *before* Thanksgiving the Christmas songs began to play all over the place and now it was three days *after* Christmas and they were still playing them. She decided not to turn on her radio or listen to any music at all heading into work. Around mid-December, she started seeing red and green in her sleep, and got tired of bumping into a costumed Santa Claus everywhere she went, along with the endless ring-a-ling of bells entering and exiting stores. Jasmine had her own private office and never learned who the charmer was that hung the mistletoe over her door post and chair. Lastly, the carefully planned lie for not being able to attend the holiday party on the sixteenth backfired, after she announced her regrets at the staff meeting. "About the holiday party everyone, I'm going to miss it," Jasmine said. She should've left it there, but she said too much. "On the sixteenth I already promised a close friend I would drive her to Sacramento that evening. She has an injury and she didn't want her elderly parents to make the drive to pick her up," Jasmine said.

"That's such a holiday spirit thing of you to do," Samantha said. "But you won't miss it, the party is on the eighteenth."

Jasmine thinks she caught that *are you kidding me* facial expression in time, but in case she didn't she decided not to say, "But I'm supposed to pick her back up on the eighteenth," and just succumbed that she would lose three hours of her life that evening. Christmas may be the most wonderful time of the year for some folks, but Simone only indulged everyone through Christmas to get to New Year's Eve, which was when the real party began as far as she was concerned. This morning though, one thing nagged at her that she suddenly recalled with the absence of music driving in. Before ending her work day the eve before, she did a quick rundown of new e-mails in her inbox to make sure there weren't any last minute urgent messages. After she was satisfied everything she eyeballed could wait until morning, she closed her Outlook, but did she see an unfamiliar e-mail address with the name Tanner in it. She was so fixated on the thought she forgot to sip on her morning coffee she made daily on her way out the door. Now, settled at her desk and logged-in, she reached for that same cup of coffee but forgot it in her car. Searching for that e-mail, she was right. "There it is tannerjasper.17@gmail. com. Could that be Simone's friend Tanner?" Jasmine thought, "And if so, what is she doing e-mailing me?" Jasmine viewed the content of the e-mail without actually opening it, in case it was something she needed to spam, but it was indeed from the friend of Simone she had been trying to meet.

> *Hello Jasmine,*
>
> *I'm Simone's friend, Tanner Jasper. I look forward to meeting you someday, but at the moment, I'm working in Florida and will not return until January. I hope you don't mind me e-mailing you, I had your address from an e-mail Simone sent out to a group of her friends awhile back. I can be long-winded, so I'll get to the point. I'm contacting you because I'm concerned about Simone and she speaks of the two of you as great friends. New Year's Eve is coming and Simone dreads it. Don't know what your plans are for the evening, but if you could just keep her in mind, I would appreciate it.*
>
> *Tanner*

"Hmm," Jasmine thought. "Simone goes to church on New Year's Eve. I think she'll be okay, but I'll see what I can do for her. I'm going to Nick's party that I know for sure. I wonder if Simone knows Tanner e-mailed me. Should I respond with a cc to Simone? Maybe Tanner doesn't want Simone to know she contacted me. I'll just reply back to her."

Hello Tanner,

It's nice to meet you, even if it is electronic. I know Simone celebrates with her church on New Year's Eve (you likely already knew that). She seems fine leading up to New Year's, but I'll see what I can do to make her feel better. Maybe I'll get her some ice cream, she says that is her go-to New Year's treat, but is that helping or worsening the problem? 😶

Jasmine

Jasmine did not want a long back and forth dialogue with Tanner. She wanted to keep things short and sweet, not pry too much or say too much like she did in the staff meeting. She certainly wanted to come across as considerate, but not overly concerned about something she did not feel was that big a deal. New Year's Eve was in one day and fell on a Saturday, so that left great time to have breakfast or an early lunch with Simone to check out her mood. Tanner already had her sexy black dress for the big party, and was getting the hair, pedi and mani hooked Friday night. She had the time to spare and always made time for a friend. When she hung out with Simone just before Christmas, it was the day of her office holiday party. She tried to get Simone to be her guest, preferring the company of a familiar friend to get her through Jingle Bells, the secret gifts exchange, and finally tasting the homemade warm cider or at least holding a cup of it around, after everyone she met asked, "Have you tried the cider, it's fabulous!" She really didn't care for warm cider, and Simone shared that she wasn't too crazy about holiday parties either, and since Jasmine had not yet attended Bible study with Simone, she didn't press the issue. Jasmine spent five days out of town with her own family for Christmas and returned the day after. Neither she nor Simone went back to work right away and caught the Bart to China Town and picked up where they left off from their last phone conversation, debating which was cooler back in the day, jumping rope or double Dutch. Hands down, Jasmine believed double Dutch was an art form and much cooler version of jumping roping. It was like how basic cheerleading just didn't seem hip anymore after you saw a classic step routine. After Jasmine's niece only requested gifts in the form of electronic gadgets, she realized how old-fashioned she was by believing a jump rope, Hula-Hoop, and Rollerblades package was an appropriate gift for an eight-year-old. "You're right," Jasmine said, "playing outside, is not as popular as it used to be. But how you rate ordinary jump roping over double Dutch floors me."

Simone believed that "you can sing better songs from jump roping because the pace is slower, plus, you can jump in and out much easier."

"Exactly," Jasmine said. "Everything about it is easier, which is why the double Dutch is cooler. You have to have skill to double Dutch. It requires technique you must master with your feet and quickness with each knee lift. If you can spin, dip up and down inside the swings *and* jump in and out without missing a beat or touching the rope you were a true double Dutch champion."

"Whatever," Simone said. "I prefer the more laid back version of jump roping." Simone did not confess that she only fancied jump roping because she never learned to double Dutch. She could never achieve the timing of jumping in between the two ropes and was always *the one* who ruined the flawless rhythm by getting tangled in the ropes when it was her turn to jump in.

They agreed to disagree and sat in the galley-styled tea saloon waiting for their host to begin. After being tasked by Jasmine, it was Simone's turn to surprise her with a unique outing for them to enjoy. She explored and discovered free tea tasting in an intimate setting with five patrons and an expert who impressed with his savvy prep of gourmet loose leaf teas. They savored a variety of fourteen different red, white, black, yellow, and green teas on the house. Once the show was over, they clearly understood why the event was free. Everyone purchased nearly all the products they sold from the teas to the china and tea making equipment. To prove she wasn't a complete bore, Simone's excursion included a foot massage and finally dessert at an adorable pastry café that boasted a European vibe. From the month prior, Simone promised she would conclude her boys to men accounts of romance or something like it, but hoped Jasmine had forgotten or was no longer interested in hearing her long-lost tales, but she didn't.

Jasmine seemed heavily invested in getting to the heart of Simone's past affiliations, hopeful that one of them lasted, even though it was obvious none of them did. As if she wanted to believe in being in love after all, as if Simone's stories were therapeutic for her somehow. Simone did not know where to pick it back up. Her teenage years were a complete fail, but Simone knew she would never forget how strongly she felt for her chief high school crush and the surprise rapport she developed with a hometown boy. His attraction to her made Simone feel terribly insecure when it should've done the opposite. Her twenties were filled with varied men who were just friends, and Simone was most relaxed with them because there were no feelings involved, so it was easy to just have fun. Then Simone met *that one guy* and she was never the same after. Finally, there was more sporadic dating and an attraction she was hopeful would bloom, but it was like double Dutch with men, too, she got tangled in the ropes jumping in and ruined the rhythm. She attempted this very short version with Jasmine including all the names of her so-called beaus to put an end to her *un*romantic relationships. "Great, that was cute. Now tell me the version with the fine points, the one with the actual details," Jasmine said. "If those men were telling the stories how do you think they would tell it?" Jasmine asked.

With that thought Simone genuinely laughed. "If they were sharing the stories, it would go something like … she was not the one, the end." They both laughed loud and hard causing everyone in the shop to look at them.

"C'mon, now. It could not have been that sad or bad," insisted Jasmine. Then she said something that made it feel like the world stopped for a moment. Simone doesn't even believe Jasmine realized she said it because of how it came out. Her body language in that second was unlike any natural expression she had ever shown. And she mumbled something, barely audible as she turned her head and rubbed the back of her neck.

"What did you say?" Simone asked, leaning in. The only words she thought she heard were "as bad" and "I." Simone knew Jasmine didn't realize her own comment after she jerked in surprise from what likely was *supposed* to be a thought but was actually voiced out loud.

"I said it couldn't have been that bad, could it?" Jasmine almost looked embarrassed, but quickly brushed off her awkward expression.

Simone didn't quite know how to respond having never seen Jasmine like that. "It was worse," Simone said. "It was worse because throughout all of it, I just ended up feeling like a looser when it came to men. And I still feel that way. Like I said before, it's mysterious and I can't figure it out." Neither could she figure out Jasmine, she thought. "I crushed so hard on Sean my entire body just felt like one gigantic heartbreak. I knew I would never be this guy's girlfriend because he was the bad boy of the school and I was the church girl of the school, which meant two things: I was invisible to everyone and I knew I had no business wanting to hook up with Sean. First of all, he had the best Gerry curl at the school, let's get that out of the way. It was moist and perfect with loose strings of curls. It wasn't one of those wet slurry ones. I like to believe we had a connection although we never had a relationship. One day at the bus stop in front of the school, he walked past me and the fluffiness from the hood of his leather jacket rubbed my arm and I thought I would pass out right there on the sidewalk. That's how ridiculous I was over him, but that wasn't the connection part. He spoke to me one time, at another bus stop closer to where I lived. I was just out walking on a Saturday afternoon and there he was. I was nervous, but I managed enough guts to not deviate from my path and go on and walk past him. I wasn't going to say anything or even look at him, but he spoke to me! I was not expecting that and from the sheer shock instead of answering his question, I just looked like a deer caught in headlights and my response was, 'huh?' He said, 'Never mind,' and he never spoke to me again."

"What did he ask you?" Jasmine asked.

"Well, I was coming from the direction where the next bus would be driving to his stop, but at the moment, it was just parked there. I obviously saw which bus it was, so he asked me if that was the 77, which I knew was the bus that took him to his apartment. What I should have said was, no, it's the 66, which was true and that could've turned out to be a great moment for us, because that meant, he wouldn't be getting on that bus and maybe we would've talked more. Anyway, the connection part came from his odd behavior. It felt like he always *noticed* me and went out of his way to nonverbally communicate with me, and this went on for three years! For example, I would be minding my own business sitting on a bench during break or lunch and I would look about and there he was with his group of friends *staring* at me. At first I thought he must be staring at someone else behind me or something. His staring made me so uncomfortable, I would get up and move somewhere else completely out of his stare stalking path, then I'd look up again and he moved too and was staring at me again. During his senior year, which was my junior year, we always crossed paths going to our last class of the day. I loved this moment because it would be my last glimpse of him as he walked south and I walked north. Well, I always walked close enough over to my right where I could get a close-up but far enough where we could not possibly collide. But as we got closer to each other, he kept moving over like he *wanted* to bump into me and he knew I was shifting to avoid the collisions. I always moved so we wouldn't hit, but one day, I made up my mind that I was not going to move this time, and I didn't and he kept scooting over and we crashed into each other. That was the only time we touched aside from his hood caressing my arm two years earlier. So, we carried on with these silly type antics until he graduated with the class of '88. There was some time during his junior year where he missed school for a spell in juvenile hall for doing something which I never found out. And one day, I'm shut-in my stall, using the ladies' room and in walks two girls and they're talking up a storm and as it turns out one of them was his pretty ex-girlfriend. What came out of her mouth about the two of them, I will not repeat. Again, he was the bad boy, I was the church girl, and what I would like to believe is he knew that, which is why he stared at me, followed me, bumped into me but aside from asking me which bus was coming that one Saturday afternoon, he never talked to me again. Although he was long gone come my senior year, not a day went by when I didn't think about Sean. The last time I saw him was probably a year after I graduated. I stepped outside of the Marshalls department store in town and he was walking through the parking lot heading toward the other side of the shopping center and I watched him until he was out of my sight."

"Did you want to go after him, call his name? See how he would respond to you?" Jasmine asked.

"I sure did, but I knew I wasn't going to, I just did what we always did … stare. He didn't see me and some days later I did wonder how he would've reacted had I called out to him. At this time, I was nineteen and he was twenty, I had, by no means, turned into some swan suddenly, but I would've liked to see his reaction to me." Jasmine seemed fascinated and despaired at the same time. Was she looking for a happy ending with one of these stories? Simone wondered. She wasn't going to get one, and Simone was still intrigued with the mumbling remark and behavior from Jasmine earlier. Maybe she would discover insight on Jasmine through sharing her stories, she just hoped it wasn't insight she would regret knowing. "During my senior year, visiting Southern Cali and my grandparents during the summer, I would see Larson for the last time and that was likely a good thing. I along with the shell I continuously locked myself in caused me to have regrets. I've heard some people say, 'I have no regrets, everything I did or didn't do was supposed to be that way.' I just learned from the experience and it made me the person I am today. I've pondered that question at different times in my life and concluded I have regrets. Even if it may have been for my good that I didn't do certain things, if I'm honest, it doesn't change the reality that I wish I had done some things or hadn't done some things. When I was thirty years old, I was just a chicken, plain and simple, for not asking the beautiful Italian, Roberto, for a good-bye kiss. We had grown to know each other as well as two professionals can during the four months he worked with my company on a special assignment from Italy. His English wasn't the greatest and my Italian was worse, but we managed to communicate with one another just fine. He was single, and I know he would've obliged me with an intimate good-bye kiss had I just asked for one. We were saying good-bye from work and he and his group were soon to depart for the airport anyway, but I froze and missed a moment that I regret. On the opposite side of that reality, I wish I had not asked that married guy out for coffee. I told my mother about this handsome fella who worked in a separate building from me, but I had to walk through his building to get to the café."

"He's not married, is he?" her mother asked.

"Of course not," Simone said. "I always look to see if a man has a wedding band, and he's not wearing one!" Simone exclaimed.

"I'd still make sure he's not married first," her mother warned.

"I know he's not married," Simone insisted. "Besides, if I started asking his co-workers about him, someone would tell him, and I'd be really embarrassed. I'm trying to drum up the nerve to just ask him out for coffee," Simone said.

"Okay, but I'd still make sure," her mother said.

"The first thing he said after I practiced in the mirror the night before and it took every bit of courage I could muster was ... I'm married. Of course, I thought of my mother, I wished I could crawl back in her womb. Thanks to God, he was not only loyal to his wife, but a complete gentleman with me. I was clearly ashamed, but he didn't get all puffed up or make me feel worse. That was the end of that, but I regret not listening to my mother. I had another regretful moment with Larson. The entire neighborhood was outside just enjoying summer. Larson was riding on a moped and had already stopped in front of my grandparents' house to say hello before zipping around the block a couple of times and making his way back. He was clearly having a hoot and on his third time around, he asked me if I wanted to ride. 'Hop on,' he said. 'I'm just driving around the block.'

'Oh, that's okay,' I said. 'Thanks, you go on.'

'Oh, c'mon, it'll be fun, I won't drive fast,' he promised.

'No, that's okay,' I said.

He smiled, shook his head and went on around the block just like he said. It was just a little ride around the block and I couldn't even do that. I wasn't afraid of the ride, I was afraid of being a teenager and doing a fun thing with a guy even though it was innocent. What was going to happen? Everybody and their mama was outside lounging, I was just a big fat square. Larson had always been kind to me since we met at ten. Since we lived so far apart, I only saw him during the holidays and summer, but year after year we became closer with each visit. I was so down on myself, I was sure he would like Sharon more than me. She lived next door to my grandparents, and he lived three homes from my grandparents, but it was me he liked. We spent our days playing together and early evenings talking on my grandparents' front porch or his front porch. Perhaps if we lived in the same zip code we would've dated, but him kissing me on my cheek was as close as we got. He was definitely progressing as the years went by, while I seemed to stay in little girl mode. By the time we were seventeen, he was an adventurous teen as I should've been, but by the time we hit our late twenties, the rumor was he had a few kids by a few different women. I sure didn't want to be one of his unwed baby mamas but I still regret not going on the moped ride."

"What's going on with him today?" Jasmine asked.

"No idea," Simone said. "His family has been gone from their home near my grandparents' for many years and someone said he moved out of the state, but I don't even remember which state it was. He sure was handsome though. Now, I was crazy about Sean, I adored Larson, but I was madly in love with Daniel. I simply loved him to pieces I could hardly stand it. I've cried to God over Daniel, had all-night pity parties over Daniel, I've prayed to God that he be okay and oh, if you could make him available God, so he could marry me, please, I would really appreciate it. Let me bump into him, let him be looking for me, let him find me, let me find him. I literally *begged* God for Daniel. I finally stopped, I mean it's been a thousand years. If he's yet with us, he's been married with a family, because that's just the way it is with me."

"Who is Daniel? All this passion and emotion for Daniel and it didn't work? How could this one have not worked?" Jasmine asked placing all the emphasis in her hands with her arms spread and looking terribly perplexed.

"Well, I didn't know him really," Simone said, and with that, she thought Jasmine would burst a vein. She nearly had a conniption.

"You didn't know him! What is it with you and these guys and your nonverbals, and we never met or we were just friends. You're killing me. Good grief, you said you were crazy in love with this guy.

What happened? And if nothing happened, why not? How could this be?" Jasmine wondered.

"Well, I didn't say he was in love with me back. That's what I've been telling you, nothing ever happened with any of these guys. Nothing *ever* happens. We meet, I find a way to blow it and that's pretty much the end of it. I met Sean, didn't I? He actually spoke to me remember? He gave me a chance at the bus stop, and I was a dork. I met Larson, we spent holidays and summers together, and I'm sure I saw him one more time after the moped incident during Thanksgiving or Christmas before he moved away. But I couldn't go for a doggone motorcycle ride with him around a block. He finally asks for a kiss and instead of landing an unforgettable mouth to mouth with him, I can't even respond to his sweet request from shock, and he yields to the second string boring peck on my cheek. With Daniel, I blew it again. I don't think he ever got over the first impression I made with him. During my midtwenties, I took some college courses and he was in one of my classes. He had this carefree look about him, but I really liked it and he seemed a bit strange too.

"Not pervert type strange, maybe a little shy type strange if that makes sense. I noticed him outside of the classroom and I was *instantly* attracted to him. I didn't think he noticed me at all, and I did not dare sit next to him in class because I probably would've forgotten how to breathe. Our instructor actually took roll call, like we were in junior high or something, but that turned out to be a good thing because then I would know his name and try out my bright idea to look and smile at him when his name was called. My other bright idea was to casually glance at everyone as the instructor called their names, as if I were really interested in my peers in hopes he would notice, so that when I looked at him, he wouldn't be surprised. It was working out. I coolly took a peek at everyone and then I thought, 'Great, he may also think I'm just really nosy.' But I was already committed to my cause, then the name Daniel was read and he said here and raised his hand. You would think I learned my lesson with Sean when he surprised me by speaking as I walked by that day but was so starstruck I couldn't even respond.

"I learned nothing. I was yet again caught off guard and yet again reacted as a young woman with zero experience winning over a young man she was fascinated with. Maybe these instances are why I don't like surprises. So, I had to turn my head left to see him, but he was positioned at a table where he could look straight ahead at me, sitting in the middle between two others. When I turned my head to look at him, the idea was to present a friendly face, show off my pearly whites and dimples, in hopes of setting myself up for an introduction during the class break. Instead, I looked at him with all the warmth of the robot you mentioned before, then I shut my eyes and turned my head back giving the impression I was rolling my eyes at him. Three things happened during that exchange. The first was the moment I looked at him, his entire body perked up as if he were pleasantly surprised I noticed him.

"The second was he actually smiled at me when our eyes met. The third was through my peripheral vision, *as I turned my head away*, I witnessed his entire face and body drop from my cold feedback. I sat there stiff and puzzled at my own behavior, and yes, that instance is the greatest regret of my life to this day. All I could think about was how I could have done that, especially after my wonderful plan. How could I make up for what I did? I have to look at him again and smile, but it was too late, first impressions mean everything and I was cut off. He showed no more interest in me. The thought never occurred to me to introduce myself to him during the break anyway. I had the perfect excuse to meet him, by trying to justify my expressions. I could've said something like 'excuse me, I think I gave you a really cold look earlier. I apologize if I did, I certainly didn't mean to, your name is Daniel, right? I'm Simone, it's really nice to meet you. But of course I did none of that. I didn't think that way then. I endured three long months in class with him never giving me a second look. It was difficult to focus and the only time I had the nerve to gaze at him was when I was certain he wouldn't see me looking. Before that quarter was ended I enrolled in the next and had a class in a huge auditorium where I saw him once. After that I saw him in the library, where I always developed the habit of going to get as much homework done as possible before heading home. I saw him in the library three times; the first was on my way out after being there for some time, the second was after I arrived and I sat on the opposite end of where he was, the third was with a group of classmates as we worked on a project together.

"That was when I had enough of my sissy attitude and decided to talk to him after I was through with the group. I took a deep breath, gathered my books and back pack and walked to his table. He was alone and I believe I asked him if he would mind if I sat here, which was across from him. He was very polite, so my hope meter turned on. I mentioned the class we had together last quarter, which probably wasn't the best idea considering what I did. I opened one of my books and pulled out a notepad and pretended to do homework. I had homework to do, but there was no way I could concentrate so I just faked working on stuff. We made small talk and this was when I saw his strangeness I told you about, but I was wrong about him being shy. I told him about a music class I was taking and he began to talk about piano playing and kind of sang out different notes, which really surprised me. Shy people don't do that with people they just met. Even now I can't explain his strangeness, except he appeared to be a loner like me.

"He was a good conversationalist, we talked about school and some magazine he loved called *Fishbone,* and I hoped and hoped that he wanted to be my friend. I hoped he would ask me for my phone number, or say, hey, let's meet tomorrow for a muffin or some-thing, but he didn't and time was winding up. There would be tons of traffic soon and if I stayed much longer, I would be stuck in the thick of it, but I didn't care. I stayed needing him to want to meet me again soon. My hope meter turned off and I began to collect my supplies and place them in my bag. I stood, produced a sincere smile, and I think I said something like it was nice talking to you. I felt completely defeated walking out and my eyes teared up quickly. He doesn't like me and he's not attracted to me, was all I could feel. I saw Daniel four more times. In that huge auditorium I spoke of earlier, where one of my classes was held, there he was already seated at an aisle desk.

"Angels began to sing, I was elated. He didn't see me and I sat two rows behind him in the middle. Shortly after class began, he gathered his belongings and walked out. What happened? Where are you going, please don't leave! I hollered in my head. Day after day, I waited for him to walk through the door and looked for him row by row in case he was already in there. He never returned and I ended up dropping this class, it was a type of boredom I would never be able to work through. I saw him next en route to my favorite course of all time, English. It was oddly quiet and it felt like he and I were the only two students on campus as I saw him walking toward me. My walking turned into floating and I wondered if I were actually lifting from the ground. I looked at him as he passed by but was unable to muster a smile because I didn't believe he liked me.

"Right after he passed me, he stopped and called out to me. I don't remember how he called out to me, just him noticing me sent me straight to the clouds. He said he remembered speaking to me in the library and I asked him about the class he left suddenly. He told me he left because he was in the wrong class and my hope meter once again turned on as I fancied the idea of me skipping my favorite class, with my favorite subject and favorite teacher. Total abandonment would've been justified at the slightest inkling of a chance to spend more time with Daniel. He then said his good-byes and I once again walked away with tears streaming down my face. Days later I saw him walking onto the campus crossing the parking lot as I was heading to my car. He wore a sleeveless sexy sport-type t-shirt that revealed a muscular tone I couldn't tell he had otherwise. I stood with concrete feet and watched him until he was completely out of my sight and after I realized who I was and where I was, I no longer had any idea which direction my car was in. I didn't know it at the moment, but the last time I saw Daniel would be the last day I attended that school. It was the last day of classes before break and again I was done for the day going toward the massive parking lot. Out of habit I looked inside a class in session as I passed the opened door and my eyes automatically lay on Daniel who happened to be in that class.

"I never slowed my walk because I didn't want to stand in the doorway like an idiot staring at him with my mouth open, but in two steps I saw Daniel sitting in his chair leaned in focused on the instructor with a pencil in his right hand and elbow rested on the desk. He wore blue jeans and his shirt was white with blue plaiting and the eraser tip of the pencil rested on the right side of his bottom lip. I could not *believe* how lucky that pencil was and would've easily traded places with it, if that was my only chance of being in Daniel's life. I wondered what Daniel would do during the school break, I then wondered what he would do for the rest of his life. That was the last time I saw Daniel and the only time I've ever been in love. Whenever I think of marriage, Daniel is the only man who enters my mind and fills my heart," Simone said.

"That is just the most awful story I have ever heard in my life," Jasmine said, and it looked like her eyes were watery.

"Do you want to cry?" Simone asked.

"I am incensed, and when I'm this angry, my eyes water. Your life is worse than the soap opera stories!" Jasmine exclaimed.

"What's it to you?" Simone asked. "Since when do you care about love and happy endings? You don't want to fall in love, but you want me to now?" Simone asked.

"It's just the opportunities were there," Jasmine said.

"See, there it is," Simone said. "You're like those people who blame me for not being married. It's all my fault, right? Perhaps, there were prospects, but it was what it was, and what I did was all I knew to do at the time. So, that's it, that's my life."

"Lies, the last guy was Tye," Jasmine said.

"Really? You really want to hear about Tye, because if you're crying over Daniel, it doesn't get any better with Tye. And I believe Tye actually liked me and was attracted to me but he dumped me too. I had to attend a five-week seminar for my job out of state and after week one, Tye asked me out. It was the football season and we got to talking about sports and there was a game on that night so we placed our picks for who would win. Since we didn't agree on who would win, he said, 'I'll tell you what. If my pick wins, I'll treat you to ice cream and if your pick wins you can treat me.' During the remaining four weeks, I really enjoyed his company, we went out and talked to each other on the phone in between our informal dates and always at the conference. We had great chemistry and I felt like I finally scored with meeting a guy where the feelings were finally mutual and he was gorgeous, this guy! He was polite, gentleman, smart. The icing on the cake was that he also traveled from California, but the cherry on top was that he worked and lived in Sacramento, just an hour from here. Can you believe that? How perfect was that?"

Jasmine covered her face and shook her head, knowing the bomb would soon drop.

"So, how I believe I blew it this time was during the final night of the conference, where a grand ball was put on by the various corporations. We would not be seated together because everyone had to sit with their own organization. There were a lot of people, at least 200. I and social settings just don't mix. I met a lot of people while I was there, and spoke to many of my peers as I searched out where my table was all dressed up at this ball, but I turned into a complete weirdo. One on one I'm fine, but back then, you put me in a shared environment with strangers and I was like a fish out of water. I felt like I was in a strait jacket and I couldn't loosen up! From head to toe I was just tense and when we finally saw each other and spoke, I sensed I wasn't the same personality he had come to know. Everything was forced and I probably looked and behaved like a frightened child needing her parents. We did not talk for very long before he jetted off, besides, dinner would begin soon and we needed to be at our respective tables. I calmed down a bit during dinner conversing with the group at my table, but I couldn't get out of there fast enough once everything was over. I was so embarrassed by my behavior I didn't want to bump into Tye again that night and hoped I would miss him on my way out to my rental car.

"Otherwise, I did think we would keep in touch for sure and arrange to meet once we got back home. Just about everyone was departing in the morning and I'm sure I thought about sending him a text letting him know I was at the airport and just wanted to say good-bye. He may have even sent me a text that morning saying good-bye, I really don't remember. I do remember he never called me again, I never called him and after about a month I deleted his number out of my phone. There, no more of Simone and her ridiculous relationships or whatever you want to call them. Those were the standout ones that I really cared about. Maybe you will enlighten me on your relationships some-day," Simone said.

"Yours have much more feeling than mine," Jasmine said. "More warmth even though they did not last. Unpredictable, that's for sure. With any of those meetings, at the beginning anyway, I would've predicted lifelong relationships. You had all the makings of a high school sweetheart, college sweetheart, or we-met-on-the-job type of sweetheart that could've blossomed into something greater, but you win some, you lose some."

"Or in my case, you lose them all," Simone countered.

"It's okay," Jasmine bounced back. "We're still better off single." She raised her coffee and clicked her cup to Simone's which still sat on the table. She kind of shook her shoulders as if she were shrugging off any attempts of romance latched on to her from Simone's stories and transported the old Jasmine back.

Those were the last conversations Jasmine had with Simone prior to New Year's Eve. She called her three times, the first while still at work just after 10:00 AM, a couple of hours after replying to Tanner's first e-mail, but there was never an answer. Simone wasn't going back to work until after the New Year, so she knew not to call her job. By 6:00 PM, Jasmine was home and she had left two voice messages. In her last one she told Simone to swing by her house, so she could show her the black dress, make them some coffee and munch on the traditional fruit cake her grandmother sent her that she was trying to get rid of. She really wanted to make sure Simone was okay. She ended up leaving work much earlier than she planned. During the holiday, a lot of personnel took off and work was slow. She also received a reply from Tanner, which she wasn't expecting at least not in the same day. As they exchanged thoughts from California to Florida, Simone became engrossed in their discussion and reveals were made at once.

Jasmine,

Hey, ice cream always helps … lol. If you get her mint chip, make sure it's Breyers. She insists they make the best mint chip she's ever tasted. Like Simone, I'll be spending New Year's Eve at church to celebrate. I found a great church to attend while I'm here.

"Really?" Jasmine thought, "Is she about to invite me to church too. Can't these girls go anywhere without church? Why did she reply back to me today? Why did she reply back to me at all? I responded to her concern. Let's just leave it at that."

What will you do for New Year's Eve?

Tanner

"I knew it," Jasmine thought. "I knew that was next. Why is she in my personal space? I don't know her. Let me put an end to this right now. Actually, I don't have to reply to her at all. This is awkward. Okay, I don't want to be rude to Simone's friend. I'll tell her my plans, wish her a happy New Year, and end it with parting words that are clear I don't want to keep talking."

Tanner,

Thanks for the ice cream tip. I will go to a friend's party on New Year's Eve. I actually threw the party at my place last year and I'm still finding bits and pieces from it. This time I'm leaving that to someone else. Well, take care and happy New Year!

Jasmine

"That should do it," Jasmine thought. She still needed to touch base with Simone and was just about ready to call it quits for the day. She looked over a file and went to update a report in her documents folder, and then Jasmine heard the ding that signified there was new mail. She didn't think much of it at first, and ignored it. Then she thought it couldn't be Tanner responding to her again and

73

tried to ignore that too. But it gnawed at her and all of a sudden there was the exaggerated feel of an Alfred Hitchcock movie with the case of the e-mail stalker or something and fear of what she would find in her Outlook. She slowly placed her file on her desk and stared down her monitor for several seconds. Jasmine went for her mouse and eyeballed her surroundings over her right shoulder as if she were being watched even though she shared her office with no one. As she clicked on her Outlook icon from her task bar, it was as if a knife would strike out once her e-mail came into view and revealed what she did not want to see, another response from Tanner. She closed her eyes and released the *you're bothering me* sigh, and just decided she wouldn't open it. But it felt too Twilight Zone. She could almost hear the ticktocks of a clock, and thought droplets of perspiration would breakout on her forehead next. As much as she wanted to disregard Tanner's e-mail, she couldn't help it, she was being drawn to it.

Well, Jasmine, the day is winding down on this end, I'm sure we'll meet next year. Likely sooner than you think. Nonetheless, I'm anticipating great blessings ahead, tolerance for those inevitable unexpected surprises and learning to live inside out. Thanks again for looking out for Simone, we talk all the time. Too much, in fact.

Tanner

"Hmm," Jasmine thought. "I wonder if she spoke to Simone today. Maybe I should've included Simone in the cc after all, maybe then I would've heard back from her by now. What do I make of this? Her message is optimistic with a pessimistic tone to it. Is she weird or is it me?" Once and for all, Jasmine was committed to logging off and jetting off, after pressing send to finally end the odd exchange of messaging with Tanner, but she made the mistake of jokingly typing her thoughts, that were supposed to stay in her head. She was too into it and her fingers were typing everything she was thinking. After she rambled on and got the cranky remarks off her chest, she continued typing the real and final message she intended to send to Tanner but pushed send before backspacing through the half she didn't mean to forward. She gasped, covered her mouth with both hands and stopped breathing for a moment. "Oh no," she thought. "I didn't do that, did I? I wasn't supposed to send that, I was just kidding, now look where kidding got me." Jasmine went to her sent folder knowing good and well she did not delete the words that were sure to offend, but had to see it to confirm it and fully accept it. With that she buried her face in her hands and thought, "Oh well, what's done is done. She's obviously at her computer and recalling messages never works, at least not for me. It's always too late. Let's see if Tanner has a sense of humor." Simone's mixed message was too contrary for Jasmine who was already a bit agitated anyway. She intended to just type:

> *You're doing better than me. I haven't been able to get a hold of Simone all day, but like I said, I'll make sure she's good to go. It was nice chatting with you Tanner. See you when I meet you.*
>
> *Jasmine*

Instead she typed:

> *Is it me or are you a complete weirdo? Your message is contradicting I don't know what you're talking about sooner than you think how do you know when we're going to meet you talk to Simone too much? and what in the hell does living inside out mean! You're doing better than me. I haven't been able to get a hold of Simone all day, but like I said, I'll make sure she's good to go. It was nice chatting with you Tanner. See you when I meet you.*
>
> *Jasmine*

"Should I wait for the reply and just get it over with? Hey, maybe I can recall it after all. I should at least try, she seemed like she was saying good-bye in her last e-mail, maybe she left after she sent it and my recall will actually work. There's a first time for everything." Jasmine proceeded to give the recall a try, but then she heard the magic ding of incoming mail. It was from Tanner. She fell back in her chair and slouched for a moment before opening the e-mail and already began composing an apology comeback in her head.

> *Wow! Simone said you weren't the type to mince words. Surely we'll meet next year, which is just a couple of days away now. I always enjoy talking to Simone, but it's not healthy to make a habit of dumping on friends all the time, sometimes you just have to talk to the Lord. The inside out reference is just something I'm going through about showing the real me and not wearing masks. Sometimes we lose the original. God takes us as we are, and then He upgrades our character, hearts, and minds so we can see, think, feel, become what He wants us to through this new original being He has transformed through our faith and obedience to Him. If we're not careful we can lose that unique work of art He redeemed. There's nothing like the original. Some things are irreplaceable, right? Just like Jason.*
>
> *Tanner*

Jasmine was completely iced and thought she could hear her heart beat. The rate and rhythm felt increased and she wondered if she would have some type of anxiety attack. Just like Jason. That was the trigger reference, which told Jasmine what Tanner wanted her to know, and there was no way she would continue their communication or go on working after that. Simone had secrets and deep seeded issues. But Jasmine had a secret of her own and it was now shredding her to pieces. If she didn't share it with Simone she believed she would literally die and then she would be doomed forever. "What comes first," she thought, "the lies or the secrets?" She had to get to her friend.

CROSS PARKER

April 15, 2006, wasn't just tax day nine years ago. It was the day Cross Parker wished he were never born. His adorned bride would soon walk down the aisle and his family and closest friends would witness the union he dreamed of and carefully planned for. Cross was no scrub. He was a professional businessman, well-educated, well-mannered, and well-rounded. Jasmine never thought he was the best looking man she'd ever seen, but he was even far from a mediocre looking man. He was Jasmine's idea of the perfect handsome. Normal handsome was a man who was not necessarily good-looking but extremely well-groomed from head to toe. Perfect handsome was not only a man who was well-groomed from head to toe, but good-looking to boot. That was Cross Parker. To make matters *better*, Cross was a Christian man. In her native Colorado, Jasmine met Cross in the parking lot of the Rivers Town Center she visited frequently for one reason or another.

This evening she required the services of Pack-it-Up and after completing her errand she dashed out, but when she got to her car parked directly in front of the shop, she realized she did not have her keys. First, she thought she left them at the mail counter, but looking inside her car, she could see them in the ignition, along with her purse on the floor, where her cell phone was. While sprinting-in-and-out on errands, she developed an awful habit of only grabbing her wallet and rushing out of the car, but she always remembered to grab her keys before she slammed the door, except this time. Now, she needed to call AAA to her location so they could work their magic unlocking her car door and that's where Cross came in. She first noticed him right after she shoved her door closed then turned opposite his direction.

77

In those few seconds, she took note of his cool walk and GQ cover attire. It was more casual than suit and tie, but so well thought out and that wine red-colored cardigan made love with his skin tone. Jasmine never gave him a second look but hoped he had business at Pack-it-Up too, so she could investigate him further. Jasmine's list of errands took over in her head, so she forgot about him sooner than later, especially since he never walked in the shop. He was just in time on his way out though. He visited the Chinese eatery two shops over, apparent from the takeout container he held in his right hand, but it was the cell phone in his left hand that inspired Jasmine. "Excuse me, could I please use your phone to call AAA?" she asked. "I locked my keys and cell in the car, it'll take five minutes."

Cross smiled at her said "sure" and handed her his cell. There was a natural calmness to Cross's persona. She immediately felt less agitated the moment he spoke and looked at her and he did not feel like the complete stranger he was. Then she realized his scent and wanted to close her eyes and dwell in it. To keep herself from weakening like Clark Kent meeting kryptonite, Jasmine made her phone call and sashayed around her vehicle while giving details to her AAA representative. Cross stood patiently by and looked Jasmine up and down in an observant kind of way. There was nothing judgmental or sexist about his glare, just common interest in an attractive woman who stopped him to use his phone. Jasmine never looked raggedy, even if her plan was to be one with the couch all day, any unexpected visitor knocking on her door would find Jasmine's appearance camera ready. She didn't go as far as Alexis Carrington's glam exterior cozied on her sofa eating caviar, but Jasmine's at-home style was a unique culture of cool, comfort, and chic.

Even out running errands she adored her heels and knew the wedge heel was most fitting for the day's activities. She sported dark blue skinny jeans with a light fitting blouse of many colors that highlighted her incredible waistline. She topped things off with her fun high bun hairstyle with loose strings of hair flirting about her face. Jasmine completed her call, which took longer than the five minutes she promised and went to return Cross's phone. "See, *fifteen* minutes just like I said. They had me on hold at first, but thank you so much for letting me use your phone. You're obviously ready to eat, so I don't want to hold you any longer." Jasmine held his phone out to him, but he did not reach back for it.

"You'll be all right here, it'll be getting dark soon, you don't need to make any more phone calls?" Cross asked.

"No," Jasmine said. "They're on the way already. I won't be waiting long." She held the phone out to him again and he still did not take it. She looked puzzled, but he just smiled at her then extended his left hand to shake hers.

"I'm Cross by the way. Cross Parker," he said. His smile had that same relaxing quality she felt from him at first, it was sincere and unforced and made the awkward left handshake feel natural. She smiled back at him it seemed at his will. His warmth was contagious and for a few moments Jasmine forgot she was still holding his phone.

"I'm Jasmine," she said. After a few seconds more, she reached out for the third time to return his cell to him and he still did not take it. "Uh, you gonna take your phone back?" she asked.

This time a barely-there laughter accompanied Cross's smile. "The blue phone book icon is my contacts. Would you mind putting your name and number in there for me? I would love to meet you again and spend some time talking to you."

Jasmine just stood there with her arm out at a complete loss for words. She knew she had a dumb look on her face and tried to grasp what just happened, so she could respond and look un-stupid as if she'd never been asked out before.

Cross chimed back in. "Is that too forward of me, Jasmine, or can you handle it?" he asked.

Jasmine put her arm down and swayed back a little. "Can I *handle* it?" she thought. Jasmine contemplated if she should feel offended, flattered, or indifferent. And again, he waited patiently as she collected her thoughts. Finally, she accepted the moment with a light laugh shaking her head. "Of course I can handle that," she said. "You have nerve, don't you, Cross?" she asked.

"It never hurts to ask," he said. "It's only the response that can hurt."

With that, Jasmine tapped the icon and placed her full name and number in his contacts. They met again in person four days later at a place most folks just don't meet on a first date ... his church. He was unpredictable in a lot of ways and made no exceptions about it. She did not expect him to be a Christian, perhaps it was the offbeat way he asked for her number. The Christian males she knew were a lot more traditional and not that spontaneous or daring. His first phone call to her was the next day, but it was at 6:00 AM. He said he figured she was a working woman and probably wouldn't mind the wake-up call, if she wasn't up and at 'em already, which she was. Instead of meeting at a movie or for coffee, he excited her about a play the drama ministry at his church worked on for three months and would present that Friday night. She couldn't wait to see it after he turned publicist selling the details of the production as told by the church announcer. Jasmine arrived at Cross's church fifteen minutes early, and he met her in the parking lot. He warned of all the stares they would receive throughout the night and hints from various members that they would make a lovely couple. But Jasmine knew all too well that scenario and filled him in on her own upbringing in the church as they hung out some twenty floors above ground on the grand rooftop of his corporate office building, another moment she certainly did not anticipate. "This is one of my favorite places to visit," he said.

They took in the lights and sights from the city beneath and soft air and diamond skies above. "Who wouldn't love this? It's pretty great up here," Jasmine said. Their communication over the last four days leading to their church play date and top of the world experience was brief albeit entertaining phone calls, from their respective jobs. He started it, after he was transferred to her direct line since he knew where she worked from his so-called wake-up call the day before.

"No one likes a happy person more than I," he said, "and if that secretary who answers phones gets any happier, she's gonna receive the Holy Ghost." That made Jasmine laugh and she was happy to hear from Cross again. "How are you?" he asked.

"I'm great, thanks, except your observation of Mrs. Katherine caused me to spill my coffee a bit. I hadn't quite sealed the lid on yet. How are you?" Jasmine asked.

"I'm great," he said. "If you haven't guessed yet, I'm a morning person."

"Yeah, I'm starting to get that," Jasmine answered.

"What do you eat with your coffee? I can never drink coffee alone, gotta have a croissant or something," he said.

"Well, ideally, cheese, tomatoes, and spinach in my scrambled eggs with a piece of toast goes fine with my coffee. But who feels like putting that together at 5:30 in the morning? Just coffee works. Do morning people like you really require coffee?"

"Not really … I don't," he said. "God wakes me up, I'm ready to go. I start talking to Him first thing! Get to work, goof off a little, check out some sports news. After that, I'm pretty enveloped in work for the rest of the day. That morning energy turns me into a work-horse until I've exhausted myself."

Jasmine and Cross would have their morning chats the rest of the week as he revealed himself a romantic. On Wednesday morning, she discovered a white canvas bag on her desk with gold-colored handles and gold inscription on the front and back which read Queen's Gold. Jasmine never heard of it, because it was a private eatery from Cross's corporate office. She pulled out a thick glossed gold Styrofoam container that looked like a briefcase. After she popped it open there was a clear plastic covering over her surprise. It was tightly sealed, but did not touch the contents, so you could see the compartmentalized breakfast as it was meant to be seen in all its morning glory. A gift of scrambled eggs with cheese, tomatoes, spinach, and a piece of toast along with a side of mixed fruit. It was all accompanied with fixings such as seasonings, butter, jam, and silverware that looked real wrapped in a gold clothed napkin.

Finally, there was a four-ounce bottle of water and a four-ounce container of orange juice. Jasmine had never seen anything like it. On Thursday, she learned it was New Friend's Day. At first, she was sure he made it up, but it turned out to really exist. It was one of those celebrated days that weren't really celebrated like Boss Day or

Loyalty Day but he used it as an excuse to flirt with her once again with a stunning green glassed rose bowl vase filled with goodies he assembled himself. There were zero fingerprints on it sitting centered on her desk, which made her not want to touch it herself and she was already thinking of great ways to utilize the vase after she emptied its fillings. Inside were a variety of everyday type needs or wants a person would use in a week's time. There was a magazine, sets of candy, packaged gum, rolls of Chap Stick, hand sanitizer, bubble bath, a latte glass mug, etc., there was even a pair of fuzzy socks. Useful things and nothing would go to waste.

When he called her that morning, he wanted to make two things perfectly clear. Number one, she wasn't special, but he did really like her and number two, he presented something similar to all of his new friends on New Friends Day. Since Jasmine was his newest friend, she was the only one who received from him. He did emphasize, however, that not all new friends received this kindness, only the new friends he *really* liked. Jasmine did not feel overwhelmed over his warm gestures after just meeting this guy. She never once thought, now what does he want in return for all of this. She was absolutely surprised, like … who does this?

It wasn't standard, but it felt like it was supposed to happen so there was no freak-out-he's-moving-way-too-fast emotions. Friday he had another surprise, but it was something he had to show her instead of send to her, thus their rooftop rendezvous after the play on Friday night. So, relaxed in cushioned chairs embraced with the excitement that comes with meeting someone new, they talked awhile and Jasmine reached in her big hand bag and pulled out two items, one in each hand. "I want to thank you for your thoughtfulness. I tried to think outside the box and get you something clever, but I failed. Here's a gift for you." Jasmine presented the gift with her left hand. "And here's the box." She held it in her right hand. "It is literally outside the box, which is as close as I could get to thinking outside the box," she said.

"Cute," he said. "Cheesy, but cute and more clever than you think. The presentation is definitely outside the box. Thank you."

"You're welcome," she responded.

"So, did you grow up in the church like me then? Born in the church? Raised in the church? Destined to be a church geek?" Cross asked.

"Is that a bad thing?" asked Jasmine.

"No," he said. "That's a great thing. I loved growing up in a family that went to church, learning about Jesus. We did a lot, we had an active youth group, a good group of kids all on the same page. We had fun," he said.

"No rebellious moments?" she asked.

"Hmm. Well, I made it through high school without rebelling. There were hesitant moments, unsure moments? I mean I was a basketball player in high school. The guys on the team bragged about a lot of things, but youth night church services wasn't one of them. All those cute cheerleaders and their pom-poms all over the place. There were times when I felt I was missing out on things but having friends from church at school helped. Now college was a different story. I lost my way a bit there for a minute and had to be reeled back in for sure," he admitted. "The Lord brought me back before I could entirely ruin my life or someone else's. You don't like to talk about yourself, do you?" Cross asked.

"Well, it sounds like my life wasn't much different from yours, except I wasn't on the basketball team and I wasn't named after the death of Jesus," she joked.

"Hey, that was my mother's bright idea," he said. "She said the cross represented joy to her and that's what I was."

"It's actually a very cool name, I like it," Jasmine said. "At least she didn't name you Jesus."

"That would've made being on the basketball team a lot more difficult," he said.

Then there was silence. It wasn't an awkward silence just a laid-back moment without words at all. Then Cross looked at Jasmine and raised his hands. "Still waiting for you to tell me more about yourself. I mean, our morning chats from work have been fun and all, but not enough time to expound on each other," he said.

"My father is the head deacon," Jasmine said. "He has been for as long as I can remember, just like my mother's been a choir director for as long as I can remember. When I was eight, our organist suddenly took ill and died. It was just a couple of months before we had another musician, but my parents decided to groom me for the future as our church musician and I began to learn how to play the organ."

Cross was intrigued with this news, and he wanted to interject and ask questions already, but chose to let her speak since she finally decided to divulge at all. "I remember the pastor anointing my hands and praying for me." Jasmine slowly rubbed her hands as she said it and then she looked at the palms of her hands. "Sometimes I can still *feel* the oil on my hands when I play. The oil is gone and my hands don't look oily or feel oily, but I can sense the oil on my hands. With my mother being a choir director and a singer and me a budding musician, that meant a lot of days and nights with my mother tapping me about different songs and notes and try this and try that. Unfortunately for me, I didn't get her singing genes. A lot of people think all musicians sing too, but we don't all sing, I'm proof of that. The pastor should've anointed and prayed for my voice too! Before you know it, I'm all grown up and I'm the church musician. Now, over the years we've had musicians come and go, and I'm not the only one anymore, we have another organist and a pianist, but I was the only one for some years through my late teens into my early twenties," she said.

"Well, how did that go over being the only musician as a teenager?" Cross asked.

"It was pressure," she said. "Like you, it felt like I was missing out on things at times. You're expected to be at all the services, anniversaries, revivals, funerals, weddings. It was a lot," she said.

"And now?" Cross asked.

"Oh, now I appreciate the gift of playing a lot more. Everything made more sense as I developed my relationship with the Lord. When I was younger I was so focused on details, learning and impressing. I played more for the church than for God. Now, I play with a much more spiritual purpose," Jasmine said.

"I've got to show you something," Cross said, "you must see this." He jumped up and pulled Jasmine by the hands. They walked about twenty-five seconds, took a turn and there stood a baby grand piano that widened Jasmine's eyes. It sung to her, and appeared to glimmer. "Of course I'm going to ask you to play it." Cross challenged.

She smiled and asked, "What don't you guys have up here? I'm not as skilled on a piano as I am on an organ, they're different instruments you know." But seeing keyboards in any form always excited Jasmine, she didn't mind playing. She sat, positioned herself and stroked through the keys to receive the feel of it. "What would you like me to play bro, Cross?" she asked.

"Your favorite song," he said.

Jasmine could never pin point a favorite song, but she did have a favorite artist, so she chose a Richard Smallwood tune and did her best interpreting it on the piano. Cross and Jasmine hung about the grand piano talking and vibing as she casually played soft chords. "What ministries are you a part of at your church?" she asked.

"The backgammon ministry for one," he said.

She stopped playing. "As in the board game backgammon?" she asked.

"First off," he said, "I don't like backgammon referred to as a mere *board game* like its checkers."

She laughed and started playing again. "Don't knock the backgammon ministry. Souls are saved using backgammon, girl. It's been a great way to get the bored kids or the restless kids specifically, into something that makes them think but they still have fun. Backgammon involves a combination of strategy and luck from rolling the dice. I present the challenge to them with the idea of considering the choices they make in their lives, just like they must choose from numerous options for moving their markers and anticipate the possible counter-move by their opponent. You can create a number of biblical lessons out of it. The roll of the dice may determine the outcome of a single game if you lucked out throwing enough doubles, but the better player, the better thinker could *still* win if he's moving and aligning his markers to his advantage," Cross explained.

"I get it," Jasmine said. "You have to be patient with the game, and cautious, it can present worldly temptations. There is the test of selfishness and greed in that game. Sometimes you always want to get your opponent if he leaves a marker open giving yourself a better chance to win, but that's not always wise. If he can break free from your hold while you have a man open, he could hold you hostage while he catches up to his side and win it all. The dice can represent the devil rolling all those doubles showing you a real good time, but the good times come at a deadly cost when you're playing with the devil."

"Very good, sis Jasmine," said Cross. "I introduce the youth to a lot of stories from the Bible using backgammon. I'll have them study the story for themselves and when they come back the next week, they share their understanding, we discuss it further, and we start up another game, I share another story and so on. At least it gets them studying the Word on their own and they begin to realize how exciting the Bible really is, even the Old Testament. They're grasping that everything they go through is already in the Bible and this is the go-to book for their problems."

Jasmine and Cross had similar lives, careers they enjoyed, Christ as their center, no children or crazy exes. They loved each other and the next obvious leap for the Christian pair would be marriage. Cross and Jasmine's courting period was filled with old-fashioned tradition, laughs, butterflies, compromise, temptation, prayer, and surprises, although the biggest surprise would be felt on their wedding day. They were both well-versed since childhood, in the ways of Christian courtship, but it was their love for the Lord and His Word and respect for one another, that banned any sexual progression. There would be no fornication, an understanding they both fully embraced from the beginning. On April 15, 2006, Jasmine and Cross were to be married. Leading up to the day was a no-fuss affair for the couple because they each had a friend who knew them well and succeeded at settling those would-be stressful details of a wedding. Loved ones anxiously gathered for the nuptials at dusk and there were smiles, hugs, lovey-dovey expressions and the sentiment that angels were present. Not a soul would have predicted the outcome. Cross and the three closest friends he chose to stand by his side would be informed at any second to make their way into the candle lit garden at the altar, styled with fully blossomed tulip heads in a breathtaking flair as opened drapes.

The gentlemen were lighthearted and reminded Cross of the pivotal basketball playoff games he would miss while on his honeymoon. Jasmine's three favorite girlfriends were nestled on the opposite end taking one last glance in the mirror before their walk down the aisle, it was time for the wedding to begin but no one had seen Jasmine in the last twenty minutes. "The bride is missing," said Sharon to Erica and Brianna. "You don't think she went to see Cross, do you?"

"No, she wouldn't do that," Erica said, "I bet she and her dad are having last words before he walks her down the aisle."

Just then Tina came rushing in to address the bridesmaids, with Emily, the wedding planner. "I gave you a simple task to keep up with the bride ladies, where is she is?" Tina was the friend from Jasmine's side who assisted putting out a couple of fires leading up to the wedding.

Before Erica could respond, Jasmine's dad walked up to the group. "Came to get my little girl, it's time." Now there were puzzled faces, but no concern just yet.

"She's here," said Erica, "we just have to find her."

"I'll check the ladies' room," said Brianna.

"I spoke to her right there in her dressing room, not twenty minutes ago just as her aunt was leaving out," said Emily.

"Was she okay?" asked Sharon.

"She was fine," said Emily. "I told her I was going to get her father and we would begin."

"The photographer," said Erica, "he was taking pre-wedding pictures of us in our dressing room, maybe he grabbed Jasmine to get some pics of her somewhere."

"We just left the photographer, he's in the main garden," said Emily.

Just then Brianna returned. "I couldn't find her anywhere, and her phone goes direct to voicemail."

"Is she with her mom?" asked Erica.

"No," said Emily. "Her mother is out there sitting on the front row. Okay, I'll put my find the bride plan into action and bring her back, excuse me." Emily turned and walked away and before she could take five steps out, she stopped in her tracks and pulled out her cellphone. She received a text, it was from Jasmine. With her back still turned to the bridesmaids she read the text and quickly phoned Jasmine, but to her shock, she found she had been blocked. She then sent her a text and that was blocked too. She took a deep breath before turning back to face the ladies and the father of the runaway bride. They all just stared at her, knowing something had gone terribly wrong. Even Jasmine's father was silent. Emily wandered back to them and presented her phone to Jasmine's father revealing the text message. He did not read the message out loud, but the ladies felt it was bad news. He returned the phone to Emily. "She blocked me. I can't get a call or text through. Why don't you give her a call, maybe she'll talk to you," said Emily.

"One of you girls go get my wife, please, and tell her to bring the cell."

Brianna took off to get Mrs. Foster. Emily would wait to see if Jasmine's parents could connect with her before heading to the parents of the groom.

Mr. and Mrs. Foster headed to Jasmine's dressing room and closed the door. They tried to reach their daughter and prayed she would speak to them, call them, text them, but she would not pick up or return their calls. It wasn't long before Donald, a close friend of Cross, whom as Tina did, stood as a liaison assuring his wedding requests, arrived at the scene of the crime to understand what the delay was. Donald was followed by the parents of Cross and soon the murmurs were heard from the garden like the growing buzz of bees gathered about a nest of honey. Cross had to be told that Jasmine was gone. He did not wait for someone to come to him despite the insistence of his groomsman that one of them would go inquire about the delay. At that point, no one could stop him from going to see for himself. It never crossed his mind for one second that Jasmine abandoned him. His fear was something awful happened. Was she ill? Had she collapsed? Did her father have a heart attack? He did not hear an ambulance, but never once did he think she was gone. Cross's mother could barely stand at the thought of how her son would take this cold news and had to sit, while Mr. Parker wanted to be the one to tell his son the woman he loved left him at the altar, but instead he could only stand there close by his wife trying to find words that would not cut through Cross's soul. No words were needed. As Cross drew closer, he saw the looks on their faces. They were not the looks of pity that something happened to Jasmine, but rather the looks of pity that something happened to him. He walked past everyone to reach Jasmine's dressing room, where the only signs that Jasmine had been present were her perfumed scent, shoes on the floor, her wedding dress draped in the arms of her teary-eyed mother and her wedding band which he noted on the vanity. After what felt like a million years of everyone standing in awe not knowing what to say to Cross, he asked, "Where is she?"

"We don't know, son, she's blocked all incoming calls to her phone," Mr. Parker said.

"How do we know something hasn't happened to her?" Cross asked.

Everyone looked uncomfortably at the other until Mr. Foster signaled for Emily to show Cross the text message. By this time the groomsmen had joined in. "I don't know what to say to you, son, I just don't," said Mr. Foster.

Cross took the phone, read the message, returned it to Emily and walked away. Heads shook, fell back, fell down, eyes closed, tears flowed, and foreheads were rubbed at the utter disbelief of the desertion of Jasmine. Cross's mother was the first to dash after him, but Lance, one of the groomsmen and best friend of Cross since childhood, interceded and assured the parents that he would go after Cross and take care of him. Mr. Parker felt that was best and conceded.

Lance was the single one of the three groomsmen and Cross's best man. He owned pretty cozy digs in three different settings, one of them would serve as a safe haven for Cross. Lance would simply see to his comfort, give him a shoulder to lean on and provide the space he needed to do whatever he had to.

The mystery of Jasmine's whereabouts continued throughout the night. She was literally curled on the floor in the estate on the grounds of the garden. Unnoticed, she dashed through an unlocked door and ran to the highest and deepest level in the estate. She had no idea which room she was in, but believed no one would even look for her there where she hid and sobbed hysterically for hours. Her head felt pinned down as if an iron ton sat on it and her head streaked of pain until it almost felt it would explode. She was utterly broken and so many thoughts passed through her mind, she could no longer keep up with them. She wanted to pass out to stop the physical and emotional suffering she was feeling. She wanted to call Cross and her parents, but mostly, she wanted to call out to the Lord, but could do neither. All she could do was lie there in her sadness, confusion, and shame because she did not understand how she could jump ship on Cross. She could not justify allowing the devil to play tricks in her head to hurt herself and the man she wanted to marry. When she woke up it was the next evening around the same time she finally cried herself to sleep from exhaustion. She could not even open her eyes and knew right away they were swollen. It just took seconds to realize her head still ached with waves of pain flowing right to left. Several minutes passed before she could roll over to put herself in a position to lift her body off the floor. Jasmine only knew three things in that moment. She had to get a message to her parents that she was alive, she would not see or speak to Cross again and she could not stay with God because she felt too guilt-ridden from her actions. Leaving the grounds of the estate was not as difficult as she thought it would be. She found employee uniforms to change into and walked right out headed to a bus stop not far from the estate. She saw a motel approaching one of the stops and would stay there. Jasmine had huge tasks ahead of her because there was no reasoning of what she felt must be done. Her mind was made up that she *had* to start a new life outside of Colorado and figure out how to leave her job in good standing on such short notice. Her boss with whom she had good relations was the only individual she met in person after arranging a very secret and heartfelt meeting with her. She was afraid of being recognized in public by anyone she knew and went through extreme lengths to alter her appearance and minimize her time out in the open. She could never even face her parents before heading to California, but managed to close details involving her wedding and honeymoon with their support. Jasmine even drove to California from Colorado to avoid any type of public transportation and being seen by anyone who knew her. She was at her lowest in life as she departed Colorado and learned how to avoid God as best she could. Jasmine invited an aggressive attitude and personality to drive her by the time she met Simone. But as she realized the tricks of the enemy in Tanner's e-mail, she could no longer avoid the pull of Christ calling her back to Him to save herself and be a witness to her friend in the process.

WATCH NIGHT

Simone wore pants to the Watch Night service, something unheard of for a girl born and raised in COGIC. She was also super late to the celebration. Not on purpose, but she struggled whether to attend at all, and then she fell asleep on her couch while debating the decision. When she opened her eyes again, it was 10:00 PM and the service began at 9:00 PM. She popped up, rushed upstairs and realized she had not put any thought into what she would wear at all, so she ended up changing clothes four times. Finally, she thought about what she would be most comfortable in that was still presentable attire and it was her navy blue slacks and blazer, so that's what she wore despite knowing it would turn a few disapproving heads. In hindsight, she really believed she wore the pants because something unbelievable would happen to her that night and if she hit the floor, well, no one would have to cover her lower body with a sheet. At last heading in to church, she felt like an overblown balloon ready to pop. Her outward temperament was collected, but on the inside, from the tip of her toes up to her scalp, she was buzzing with a corrupt type of energy that would not cease. After she walked in the main sanctuary, she was stunned that Jasmine was the first person she noticed.

She stood in such shock, the usher touched her arm to bring her back to earth. Jasmine sat on the end of the pew, third row from the back. They recognized the troubled look each one had on their faces staring at each other. Jasmine signaled for Simone to sit next to her as she made room on the pew. Neither spoke to the other, but Simone looked at Jasmine wondering if she had realized her secret or if she finally just accepted Simone's invitation to join her at church. Simone knew how much Jasmine was looking forward to Nick's party, so she assumed it was the former. She then also grasped how out of touch she had been with outsiders, the last several hours. Simone had no idea where her cell was or if it was even turned on, she just knew it wasn't in her purse because she changed purses to match her outfit. And she knew it wasn't in her car because she rushed out with just her purse. She didn't even have her Bible or think to grab the car Bible she kept in her back seat pocket. Jasmine did not begin any type of dialogue with Simone, she just looked straight ahead and turned her attention back toward the service. Simone missed all the singing, testimonies, and short sermons from the missionaries and elders. The pulpit had turned the service over to the pastor where he would have expressions before praying and everyone would praise God right into the New Year.

When that moment arose some were on their feet, others on their knees and it was electric. Simone stood there with her head bowed, eyes closed, and hands clinched to her mouth. She could feel the joy in the voices of the praises surrounding her but could not break free to enter them. Simone wanted to praise but she was thinking too hard on her uneasy feelings. As tradition goes for Watch Night, after God safely escorted the congregation into a New Year, and the praises lightened, they would break out in song, hug and greet one another saying, "Happy New Year." The pastor would pray for *each* family, the benediction would be spoken and everyone would gather in the dining room to enjoy a meal of some sort. This year chicken and waffles were served, but Simone would not be a part of any of that. She found she was boxed-in stiff into her own world and knew she was the only one still standing even though her eyes were closed. She started another testimony service even though she would be the only one to testify this time.

Simone refused to open her eyes as the sanctuary grew silent and she felt all glares on her. If she opened her eyes, she would see the faces of the people and feared she would panic like Peter did after he turned his focus on the storm around him instead of staying centered on Jesus ahead of him walking on water. She felt with her eyes closed she could allow the Lord to bless her to say what she needed to say, so she could feel what she needed to feel and begin the deliverance process from all of the mind tricks the devil pulled on her for being single.

As Jasmine realized Simone would speak, she stood with her, but did not touch her. She could see herself in Simone in that instance after she ran from her groom, lying on the floor desperately wanting to call out to her family, Cross, and the Lord on her wedding night, but could not. She knew Simone was struggling to get her words out, struggling to defeat the devil and his lies, but she would speak out eventually and Jasmine wanted to stand by her side as she did.

The saints began to pray for her aloud and the pastor began to encourage her to speak. She still kept her eyes closed, held on for dear life to the pew in front of her and said, "Finally, brethren, whatsoever things are true, whatsoever things *are* honest, whatsoever things *are* just, whatsoever things *are* pure, whatsoever things *are* lovely, whatsoever things *are* of good report; if *there be* any virtue, and if *there be* any praise, think on these things. I have not thought on the truth, I have thought on lies and fantasies and become someone I am not. The-devil-is-lies! Tanner is not real, Tanner is not my friend, Tanner does not exist! I am Simone, just Simone and I need the Lord to deliver me from the lies, from the sadness, to His truth, to His joy. I just want to be me again in God through Jesus and the Holy Ghost!" Simone confessed her imaginary friend, her sins, her faults, her weakness, her *heart* in the Watch Night service. She cried out for help disclosing personal demons and the church embraced her courage and showed love and understanding toward her testimony.

Simone stomped her feet and pounded her hands, she went for broke as they say, caring more for her soul during that moment than anything else. It was a good thing Simone wore the slacks. By the time she was done, she had run up and back from the altar, hit the floor, did a little rolling, her legs were expressive but she was experiencing freedom and truth in that moment and her body moved within her emotions. Would there be the judgmental few who would take this story and run to the gossip mill? Sure, no church was perfect, there were others who needed to be delivered and everyone who attended church was not saved unto God. Bro. Glynn and his wife Lynda attended the Watch Night service, as guests and friends of the

Clarke family, who were members. The Glynn's worked in psychiatric therapy and were advocates for treatment and during their off-time spoke at churches simply to admonish the saints not to dismiss therapy because they were children of God. He once said, "Often times as saints, we may feel we are letting God down for choosing to go to a doctor or God forbid a physiatrist. Why should we use these resources when we have one-on-one contact with God through Jesus, or the Holy Ghost He has given us? On the spiritual side, we have to *learn* to pray, we have to learn our new lives in Christ and on the natural side, we sometimes have to *learn* to talk things out to get to the source of a problem we have that could grow out of control otherwise. It doesn't mean you don't believe God, it could mean you're not as strong in an area of your life as you should be or thought you were and the right type of therapy could lead you to discovering things about yourself you may not have been aware of. It's similar to when you may have thought you were good and saved and on the right track in the Lord, then He allows you to go through trials and suffering periods and you realize you were not as committed to the Lord as you thought you were. Sometimes He allows us to go through trials to show us ourselves and what areas we need to grow in. Therapy is another way to discover some things about yourself that you never realized. It's about honesty, communication, and coming to terms with the truth about conflicts in your life. It may not be for everyone, we're all different, but if it could help you, why not give it a chance? It's a basis God has made available for us."

Bro. Glynn could not keep his seat witnessing Simone's testimony he was personally moved and responded quickly making arrangements to at least have her endorsed for proper treatment. Simply, she would benefit greatly through the right form of psychotherapy once a week until she felt stronger, mentally, emotionally, and spiritually. The devil would even speak lies to her about how others would now view her after she exposed such a personal secret. Was she cuckoo? Would they now think she is cuckoo? The devil would try to make her think so.

Simone was already mentally drained leading to her Watch Night reveal. Now that she let it all out, her body collapsed. She was not completely unconscious, but certainly not coherent and would not be driving home on this early New Year's morning as she had year after year, first stopping at some grocery store to claim her favorite ice cream treat. This time, she woke up in a strange place with some woman and her tarantula eyes hovering over her, but she felt at ease in her spirit. Not like before when she believed she would have an anxiety attack. "How do you feel, Ms. Rinney?" asked the nurse.

Simone thought about it for a moment really wondering how she felt. "I feel thirsty," she said.

"I'll get you some water then," said the nurse.

"Where am I, exactly?" asked Simone.

"The emergency room at Missions Memorial Hospital. You have some family and friends out there. They were in here with you earlier, but it's not much room in here, so they went back out to the lobby, would you like me to go get them for you?" she asked.

"Not really, I'll just take that water, please," said Simone.

"Be right back," said the nurse. "The doctor will be in to see you though."

"Sure," said Simone. She began to remember everything that happened and that it was New Year's day. She did not quite know what to expect next, but she felt a sense of liberty and relief but she also felt embarrassed and knew that facing everyone would be a challenge. She sat up slightly in her bed wondering what her next move should be, she just wanted to go home. She observed her identification wristband and the hospital gown she was in and became a bit weirded out that she did not recall being swapped into a gown. She was relieved her pants were still on and it was only waist up clothing missing. She didn't think her episode called for all that, but she was in the ER after all. She could not tell what time it was behind her sectioned area, but hoped it was still early New Year's day and not the second. As she thought on these things the nurse returned with the water, but Simone was ready to ditch her hospital visit. "Thanks for the water," Simone said. "What time is it, please?"

"It's just after 4:00 AM," said the nurse.

"Oh, well, I'm feeling better and I'm ready to go. What do you need from me for discharge?" Simone asked.

"You'll just have your consult with the doctor and sign your discharge form. Your parents provided us with everything else," the nurse said.

Simone nodded and decided to put the rest of her clothes on while waiting for her doctor, who went through all the necessary release processes. Her parents surfaced shortly after the doctor because the nurse told them she was prepping to leave. Jasmine was still there, too, but she waited out in the lobby with Bro. Glynn and his wife, who insisted on staying so they could meet Simone and arrange an appointment to introduce her to some recovery programs. They were relieved she was willing to meet them and discuss options. She was also happy to see Jasmine who greeted her with a hug. Jasmine thought she was there for Simone, but God was showing His grace toward Jasmine through Simone. She knew she needed to return to Him. "Girl, do we have lots to talk about," said Jasmine.

"I know," said Simone. "Thank you for being here. You didn't have to stay."

"Of course, I did. That's what friends do. You look really good for someone who passed out, you know," she said.

"You know, I feel wide awake now and I feel good, too," said Simone. "But once I get into my own bed, I'm sure I'll fall into seven-level sleep."

Jasmine sighed. "After you get your rest and feel up and at 'em, give me a call. It really is my turn to share a lot of things with you now. There is a lot you don't know about me," said Jasmine.

"You're not really a man, are you?" Simone managed a lazy laugh.

"Oh, that's good you have jokes," said Jasmine. She gave her another hug and said, "I'm glad you're okay. We're both going to be okay now."

Simone was not sure what she meant by that, but she could tell her parents were not only ready to get her home, but they were ready to go home themselves.

"Hey," said Jasmine, "when I come over I'll bring some mint chip ice cream for us. Breyers, of course."

Simone nodded. "Thank you," she said.

Simone's father drove her car to the hospital from the church and then followed Mrs. Rinney and Simone to her home from the hospital. They wanted Simone to go home with them or either stay with her until later in the day, but she convinced them she was fine and would be okay at home alone. She knew she would have a heart-to-heart with them at some point about Tanner, but they were not the pushy type and allowed her space to come to them when she was ready. Simone did fall into a deep sleep zone after she settled at home and woke up four hours later. She approached God on her knees with her upper body slouched over an ottoman. She thanked Him and talked to Him about the last several hours. She asked Him to help her hear and receive how He would have her to continue healing from this experience. She did not wish to be a sad single woman always wondering if she would be married and if every guy she met was the guy. She wanted to be joyful and content the way she was. There was such a need to glorify God, and follow His lead on all the things He would have her to do to honor Him, and her Savior, Jesus Christ. Her life was in His hands, and she went back to her motto of living in Christ one day at a time. "Lord, I can only live in the very moment that you give me. Tomorrow is not here yet and yesterday is gone. Help me to live for you today, just get through today. I used to talk to you about everything, I'm going back to that. I used to be more patient waiting for you, listening for you to talk back to me. I'm getting back to that too. I put Tanner in your place because she told me what I wanted to hear, but you'll tell me what I need to hear." Simone studied scriptures and felt encouraged and comforted by the Word of God. She received the expected call from her parents who checked in on her and after a glass of orange juice and a bowl of green grapes Simone called Jasmine for her visit.

She listened to Jasmine share her personal story of receiving Christ, love, loss, regrets, rejecting Christ, and accepting Him again through Simone's trial of Tanner. They talked, cried, confessed, and prayed. "Will you ever speak to Cross again?" asked Simone.

"I won't feel settled in my spirit until I do," said Jasmine. "I just want to apologize to him, tell him how sorry I am for being so cruel and hurting him. I don't have the courage to meet with him face to face though, so I don't know how I'll tell him, but I've asked God to help me find a way to do it. I wanted to marry him, it was just fear minutes before the ceremony that just blindsided me and froze me, turned me into a complete coward. It just came from out of nowhere, I don't know if I'll ever understand it."

"I'm just going to say this because I have to," said Simone, "it's what I'm thinking so I'm just going to tell you. He might still be waiting for you, you know."

Jasmine shook her head. "I am a complete mess when it comes to Cross and the idea of marriage, period. The only thing I need right now is to continue my relationship again with the Lord. I have issues. First, I feel like Cross is too good for me. Second, I have this fear that if I did decide to marry, the man would do to me what I did to Cross. The way I feel right now, I would never have a ceremony again and risk being left at the altar, but I'm so paranoid, even if I decided to elope I fear he would ditch me for that too. I'm a long way from thinking about marriage again. I'm sure Cross has moved on, I hope he has. I nearly had the biggest diva moment, major conniption, and panic attack all rolled up in one, when my parents tried to give me an update on Cross at different times the last few years. I acted out so badly making it clear that I want to know nothing about Cross, no one in my family dare mentions him to me. I don't know what's going on with him, I just know he shouldn't be with me," said Jasmine.

"Yep," said Simone, "you're messed up." They were able to laugh a little reflecting on Jasmine's observation of herself. "I encourage you to adopt my motto for living in the will of the Lord. One day at a time. Just get through the day at hand with Him. Are you afraid of getting back into church?" asked Simone.

"No. I felt very comfortable at your church, I'll visit again, I'm going to find a church home. How do you feel about going back to church?" asked Jasmine.

"Hmm. I don't know if afraid is the right word," said Simone. "More like embarrassed or nervous. I had to do it, I had to get it all out. I didn't know I would, but the moment was there and I couldn't keep silent. I had to be delivered from Tanner. She wasn't like a demon from the *Exorcist* or something, but she was an idol, and who knows what she could have become in me if I had not broken free from her. It's not safe to entertain unhealthy thoughts."

"Are you going to talk to that doctor, the guy from the church discussed with you last night?" asked Jasmine.

"I don't want to be dependent on doctors, I want to be dependent on God. But I am interested in speaking with him, see how it goes," said Simone.

"When you go to church again, I'll go with you maybe that will make you feel better," said Jasmine.

"It will make me feel better. And I'm going right back for Bible study on Tuesday, I'm just staying right in. I love Bible study and I don't want to stay away from something I love just because I told everybody I had an imaginary friend who took over my life. And thank you for going with me. I appreciate that," said Simone.

BENEDICTION

“How's Tanner?” Simone's doctor asked. It was therapy day and this was her first visit with Dr. Nelson some eight days after Watch Night. They kicked things off with great first impressions. Simone felt very comfortable and all was going well with their back and forth until that question. She felt a little trapped in by it, like a mouse hiding in her sheltered space seeing that peanut butter ahead, but wondering if she should go for it.

“Is he testing me? How is he expecting me to respond to that?” she thought. Simone could only look at the doctor for a moment and felt a little hurt that he would even ask her that question. “Is he being a smart mouth?” her thoughts continued. “I don't need a smart mouth doctor, he's supposed to be helping me not bringing up bad memories.” Simone looked down fiddling with her nail, and then she looked away at the art about his office. When she turned back at him to look in his eyes, she was ready to respond. “Tanner isn't real, Mr. Nelson. I haven't allowed that image I created of Tanner to dwell in my being since New Year's Eve. I thought about her a few times, but every time I did, I started praying to God so I wouldn't be distracted with thoughts of her,” she said.

“It's as easy as that?” asked Dr. Nelson.

“It's the praying part that's easy because my mind is made up that I don't want to feel blogged down with thoughts of Tanner again,” said Simone.

“How did you communicate with Tanner?” asked Dr. Nelson.

Another question that made Simone feel awkward. “What does he mean, like did I pretend to call her on the phone or something?” she thought. “It was all in my mind, in my head,” Simone said. “It was just a dialogue between me and someone named Tanner, but it

101

all happened in my head. I didn't speak out loud and then answer out loud, it was silent, but very distinct, very specific if that makes sense."

"What did she look like?" asked Dr. Nelson.

Simone looked surprised. "You know I … I never truly gave her a face or a body. She didn't look like anyone really. I only saw myself, I guess she looked like me, a stronger version of me," said Simone.

"But you gave her a name. A face didn't come with the name? Where did the name come from?" asked Dr. Nelson.

"There was no face other than mine. The name was just a pretty name I always remembered from hearing it for the first time years ago. Just thought it was really unique and never forgot it. Thought it would be a great name for a little girl if I ever had one. It just stuck with me," said Simone. "I just wanted to encourage myself. Instead of encouraging myself in the Lord, like David did, I encouraged myself in someone I named Tanner. She was a lot like me, except she was a military woman, she was in the Air Force. I don't know why I made her a military member, it seemed cool, it seemed fitting. And she was single like me, I even made her a Christian, but unlike me, she was not anxious to be married. She was happy the way she was. She didn't feel any pressure to marry or feel like a freak because she wasn't," said Simone.

"If you were anxious to be married and you created this woman as an alter ego, why didn't you make her married?" asked Dr. Nelson.

Simone seemed lost for words and ran her hand over her forehead scratching her head along the way, as people do when they don't know what else to do. Finally, she said, "Good question. I don't know, I have no idea. Maybe because, uh, I don't know what it's like to be married, so I couldn't, um, have her communicate back to me as a married woman." Simone shrugged her shoulders.

"Well, have you ever been in the military?" asked Dr. Nelson.

"Nope," said Simone.

"But you were okay with Tanner being in the Air Force, which is something you also never experienced," said Dr. Nelson.

"Well, I know people in the military, I've talked to people in the military and they've shared their experiences," said Simone.

"Do you know married people and have they ever shared their experiences being married?" asked Dr. Nelson.

"Yes," said Simone. "Dr. Nelson, I don't know why I did not have Tanner a married woman. Hanging out with married women when you're single just isn't ideal, maybe that's why."

"I said you were anxious to be married from your own comment about yourself, are you still anxious to be married?" asked Dr. Nelson.

Simone closed her eyes and thought about that question for a moment until she let out a nervous lazy chuckle. "Mentally and emotionally, I've exhausted myself on the topic of marriage as it pertains to me. I don't wish to dwell on it any longer. I don't know if I want to be married anymore. I just know I want to be right with God and I can't be right in the eyes of God pretending to be someone I'm not or trying to make myself feel better through someone who is not even real. I'm anxious to live my life as myself the way God intended. I don't know what all He has in store for me, but I know one day at a time, I'm going to find out, without Tanner," said Simone.

"Has anything good come from this experience?" asked Dr. Nelson.

"God's grace, God's love, God's forgiveness, His patience. A number of things. The fact that I was able to follow Him and obey as He was leading me to confess my sins and break free from Tanner. The fact that my friend Jasmine returned to the Lord through all this. It shouldn't have ever happened in the first place, but since it did and I'm healing from this, now I'm seeking to find what other good conclusion will come from it myself. How do I live as a single Christian woman? Because that's what I am … a single woman striving every day to live according to God's Word. One day at a time, I will come to terms with that in the Lord. Because the truth is, I may never marry," said Simone.

She and Dr. Nelson continued their sessions for one and a half months. They met once a week, sometimes twice in seven days. He asked a bunch of questions and she answered. At times he offered suggested *possible* solutions, but clearly forced her to dwell on his questions and understand her response and feelings about those questions and answers. Over time, she would think about the boys in her life and men she dated in the past and of course she thought about Daniel, whom she always believed was the one who got away. Eventually, she would *rarely* think of Daniel at all. Even if someone mentioned Daniel from the Bible or she was studying the book of Daniel, *her* Daniel would not cross her mind unless it was one of those *by chance* moments, like if she heard the name of the school where she met him, or a song called "Heaven" by Bryan Adams. Simone doesn't know why she thought of Daniel when she heard that song, the few times they spoke there was never music playing anywhere around. It's a beautiful song, but sometimes when it played on her Pandora soft rock station, she had to skip to the next song or another station she created.

In time, Simone's thinking was converted from *why am I still single* to just live as you are and embrace that way of life. But the most important concept she grasped was that marriage is not for everyone and with that came even greater peace about being single. She realized the idea of marriage, just like with most girls, was highlighted in her mind ever since she was a child. It was a natural expectation to grow up, get married, and give her parents grandchildren to spoil. She thought about all the times she heard since she was a child "one day you're going to get married and start a family of your own" or as she grew into her teens "you'll meet a great man to marry someday" and finally in her mid-twenties and on ... "you're next!" When marriage did not happen for her there were a lot of anticipated dreams she had to rid out of her mindset and insecure feelings she would need cleansing from. The Bible is written of man and woman, multiplying the earth, and how it's not good for man to be alone, but it doesn't read he or she would not be alone.

The big promise Simone clung to on never being alone is the one where God promised *He* would never leave her alone. Simone was not that woman who claimed Jesus as her *husband*. That was not His role, He is the husbandman to the church as a whole, that's scripture ... and He was a number of things to Simone, but a husband was not one of them. Simone never knocked marriage. She witnessed healthy and loving marriages in her family from her parents to her grandparents. Simone never believed she did not *need* a man. She simply did not have one, so made the best of her life single.

If Simone were honest, the only thing that saddened her from time to time was never having children. Not ever having children out of wedlock, but never having children as a product of marriage. She loved having a married mom and dad growing up and did not wish to have a child without a husband. That was a deal breaker as they say and a very personal choice she was committed to, even though it caused great tears and sent her running to Jesus for comfort over a period of time.

Simone and Jasmine became best friends, but Simone never pressured Jasmine into dating or bugged her about getting in touch with Cross. She did let Jasmine know that she prayed her feelings about herself would change in terms of believing she was banned of ever being in a relationship again because she left Cross at the altar and the fears she held as a result of that. Simone and Jasmine were excited about the San Francisco Street Food Festival again.

This time two years ago, they were both pretty messed up and they knew it. They enjoyed another new year with new lives, so they strolled from block to block munching on delicious art in small plates and bowls. They found themselves at the same park people watching and relaxing afterward. "I feel like I see people differently now," said Jasmine. "People look happier to me than they did before. Sometimes I can see that a person is struggling with something, but mostly because I'm happier, I don't see as much gloom in others as I used to. Even in someone else's sadness, I still see hope and try to encourage them if I can. Geez, I'm so grateful the Lord didn't let me see death in my sins."

"Me too," said Simone, "If you had given up the ghost, I wouldn't be picking up my new car in two days. I reaped a raise networking through your fancy corporate peers for my new modern knowledge!"

"You still say funny things," replied Jasmine.

"No, seriously, Jass … you've started some really great things that help people spiritually and naturally—your Networking Initiative, and Lives Learning the Lord. But I can't wait to pick up my new wheels. It's being specially painted in my favorite color, green," said Simone. "Hey, speaking of your peers, please tell me you contacted that guy Phillip something. The young man almost looked like he needed his mother's permission to work, but he's super smart. He was with the group that visited my office and asked me to let you know he's been trying to contact you. His last name starts with a B."

"Barnes, Phillip Barnes, I did finally get in touch with him," said Jasmine.

"Good," Simone answered. "He said he never had such a hard time finding another employee who worked in the same building and wondered if you really worked there."

"Yep, I was starting to wonder the same thing about him," said Jasmine. "But I was always in some meeting or out to lunch, missed his call, or he just missed my call, plus, he works different hours. He wants to be a part of the backgammon ministry I'm starting."

"Yes, he shared that with me," said Simone. "I told him he's gonna have to talk to you about that, *but* if he wanted to be a part of my football pool he was in. Bragging rights only, we don't play for money."

They took a moment of silence to finish off dessert treats they nabbed from the festival and observed a guy getting his guitar ready to play for his audience of laid back park settlers and passersby hoping they would dish out a few bucks in his bright nifty basket. "I noticed you don't talk about marriage the way you used to Simone. We don't talk about a lot of things we used to actually," said Jasmine.

"I don't think or talk about marriage the way I used to because I don't feel the same about being single as I used to. You know, I've always been happy for others who fall in love and get married. I'm just victorious in my life as it is. To marry or not to marry, it really is a choice you know, just like choosing to be in God's will or out of it. These days the opportunities to marry are out there if you really want to. I just understand now that marriage isn't for everyone. The other day I was listening to a Christian radio broadcast and this preacher spoke from a scripture passage in Genesis that tied to my past way of thinking and behavior. It speaks of Cain and his issues, let me pull it from my iPhone." Simone tapped her Bible App and went to

Genesis chapter five and started at verse six. 'And the LORD said unto Cain, Why art thou wroth? and why is thy countenance fallen? If thou doest well, shalt thou not be accepted? And if thou doest not well, sin lieth at the door. And unto thee *shall be* his desire, and thou shalt rule over him.' Remember Tanner? I did not do well. I became bitter at times, angry at times, a bunch of different emotions and my countenance fell. She became the sin that lied at the door. I allowed the imagination of perfect Tanner to rule over me instead of what God said that I should rule over sin. I am an older unwed Christian woman with no children and I used to feel like some sort of freak because of it. I never spoke that out loud, but in my mind I said it over and over again. I used to call myself a weirdo because I wasn't married. Now, I'm delivered from those evil thoughts, now I feel normal. God has a plan and use for those who will never marry. I'm single and for the first time in years I feel *un*weird about it."

ABOUT THE AUTHOR

A ngela Beverly is a Compton, California, native. Military orders allowed her to experience overseas adventures as a child, but ultimately, she and her family settled in northern California's Bay Area. She coincidentally followed in her father's footsteps and joined the United States Air Force and even landed in the same career field, as a communications and information manager. Unlike most, Angela enlisted at the age of twenty-five and marked her choice to serve as one of the best decisions she's ever made! After twenty years of honorable service, Angela retired as a technical sergeant in 2016. She seeks to grow daily in her spiritual walk with the Lord, and relish the company of her family, friends, and sports.